D0765242

TITHING
THE LORD'S LAW

ROY W. DOXEY

TITHING
THE LORD'S LAW

Published by
Deseret Book Company, Salt Lake City, Utah, 1976

DEDICATION

To my helpmate of over forty years, mother of our children.
Her faith and devotion to the gospel of Jesus Christ have been
a constant strength in sustaining me in my opportunities
for service in the Church.

ISBN 0-87747-615-2
Library of Congress Catalog Card No. 76-41587
Printed in the United States of America

CONTENTS

PREFACE

When The Church of Jesus Christ of Latter-day Saints was organized on April 6, 1830, the embryo kingdom of God was born. Over the years this kingdom has grown steadily. Evidence is mounting that it will eventually fill the earth, as prophesied by ancient and modern prophets. Since it is a restoration of the eternal gospel of Jesus Christ, it will in time replace the false religious beliefs and practices that have enveloped the world for centuries. Its impact has been felt in the world, not only in the realm of doctrines, but also in the application of those teachings. Ancient truths enunciated in gospel dispensations before the time of Christ and renewed with the Savior in the meridian dispensation have vitalized the lives of millions of adherents of the restored church.

Important factors contributing to the success of the true church include: (1) the possession of divine authority, the priesthood, which is God's authorization for success in the lives of those who want to be one with him; (2) revelation, which is received by those who do the will of the Lord; and (3) a church that is led by a prophet who receives the mind and will of the Lord for its direction.

These truths explain the reason for the many distinctive teachings and practices of The Church of Jesus Christ of Latter-day Saints—distinctive because they are different from the beliefs of the so-called Christian world and because they are vital and life-giving. Among these practices is that of tithing, the payment of one-tenth of one's interest or income to the Church. Voluntary contributions to this revenue raising program of the Lord's church is the obligation of each member, together with other free-will offerings, which, when combined, provide the revenue to keep the kingdom of God growing.

By way of contrast, a news magazine recently reported on the situation of the Church of England, which does not have tithing, the Lord's authorized revenue plan. It was reported that one parish in England, St. Barnabas, serving 13,000, had fewer than twenty parishioners who attended Sunday services regularly. The vicar of that parish said, "We have lost hope. The church is mortally wounded. The service is meaningless to outsiders. The only time they need me is when they are dead." The article maintained that this parish's disintegration was typical of the Church of England. At least $190 million would be needed to operate the church in 1976, but only $80 million was expected to be received from investments. The church has experienced a decrease in membership from 3 million to 2 million in twenty years, with only 13,000 clergymen today, 2,500 fewer than in 1969, and an estimated loss of 3,000 by 1980. Contributions by collection in an Easter service in one of the largest parishes netted only about $35. (*Newsweek*, November 17, 1975, p. 70.)

The Lord's plan for his church is the law of tithing and other offerings. Some individuals outside the Church have tithed their incomes to be distributed to charities of their own choosing because their churches did not require it of them. Elder James E. Talmage observed that some churches have tried to institute this law in their organizations, but success is determined by the administration of the law of tithing by the Lord's authorized priesthood. (*The Articles of Faith,* p. 526.)

This book was written to explain the law of tithing and other offerings for investigators of the true church, for members who have not yet developed sufficient faith to live the law, and to strengthen the determination of tithe payers to endure to the end. Finally, through the medium of this book I am afforded an opportunity to bear personal witness that temporal and spiritual blessings come to those who seek to live this law and other principles of the gospel of Jesus Christ. The soul-satisfying knowledge that one is on the Lord's side, contributing to the advancement of his church, and assisting in the preparation for the eventual establishment of Zion upon the earth is ample payment for obedience to the law of tithing and other offerings. Since I have become a wage earner, temporal and spiritual blessings have been bounteously received because of obedience to this law. The Lord's promises are fulfilled. "But seek ye first the kingdom of God, and his righteousness; and all these things shall be added unto you." (Matthew 6:33.)

Appreciation is expressed to Nancy McCleve and Eloise Godfrey for their assistance in typing this manuscript.

1
THE LAW OF TITHING

"I preach that which I believe and that which I do know to be true, and I do know that if men will obey the laws of God, God will honor and bless them. I have proven it all my life through. I saw it manifested in circumstances which occurred in my childhood, and I know that God has blessed the widow and the fatherless when they have been obedient to his laws and have kept his commandments." (Joseph F. Smith, *Gospel Doctrine,* p. 230.)

When Joseph Smith declared that he had been visited by God the Eternal Father and his Son Jesus Christ in the spring of 1820, the promised restoration of the true church of Jesus Christ had begun. By divine commandment, the Church was organized on April 6, 1830, with only a handful of people present. From this small beginning the Church is today one of the fastest-growing religious organizations in the world.

The Church of Jesus Christ of Latter-day Saints is acknowledged by many as being different from other Christian religious bodies. It is distinctive not only in its teachings, but also in the loyalty of its members to their beliefs and their leaders. From the day the Church was organized, some form of persecution has been leveled against it. This persecution was most evident during the century of its birth and in the early part of the twentieth century. During the past few years, however, people have begun to learn more about the Church and thus to change their views. The First Presidency issued a message in which they made this observation and then added:

" . . . In fact this recognition has taken the form, among some of the Christian sects, of adopting certain principles of the gospel taught by the Church: The principle of revelation, the doctrine of the personality and individuality of the Godhead, the law of tithing . . . and other principles revealed by the Lord to the Church." (James R. Clark, *Messages of the First Presidency,* Bookcraft, 1965, 4:207.)

One of the most distinctive practices of The Church of Jesus Christ of Latter-day Saints is observance of the law of tithing,

2

which requires a member to give one-tenth of his increase to the Church. Keeping in mind the fact that the priesthood held during Old and New Testament times was restored as a vital part of the Church, the following point made by Elder James E. Talmage is significant:

" . . . during recent years, particularly during the two decades last past, attempts have been made by many sects and denominations to revive the ancient practice of the tithe. Churches are organizing from among their members societies or clubs of 'tithers', who voluntarily pledge themselves to pay to their respective churches a tenth of their individual incomes. Among some of these societies the tithers are permitted to indicate the purpose to which their contributions shall be applied. The great difficulty which our sectarian friends find in reestablishing the practice of the tithe amongst their numerous sects is—and they realize it in part—that they have no priests or Levites amongst them authorized to receive the tithe and administer it strictly in accordance with divine command. The authority of the Holy Priesthood is essential to the regulation of the tithing system of the Lord." (*The Articles of Faith,* p. 526.)

Successful tithing practice is not dependent only on God's priesthood; there must also be dedication to the fulness of the gospel, in order to bring about compliance to this voluntary tithing principle. Although not all of the members of the Church are tithe payers, the number is increasing as faithful converts are baptized and older members rededicate themselves to this important principle. The faith of one humble member demonstrated in the following account by Elder Robert L. Simpson, Assistant to the Twelve, is just one example of such dedication:

". . . I shall always remember the faith of an old Maori brother in New Zealand. As the missionaries came to his humble little fishing shack located well off the beaten track, he hurried to find an envelope that contained a letter addressed to him and in which he had also stuffed a sizable sum of hard-earned money. He promptly handed the envelope containing the money and letter to the missionaries. This fine brother didn't have the ability to read the letter when it arrived, for it was written in English and his tongue was Maori, but he could read the financial figures contained in it, and he recognized the letterhead as being from the mission office. He thought the mission needed the cash amount mentioned for some special purpose, and he had it all ready for the missionaries. After translating the letter for him, it was now clear that the letter merely confirmed his annual tithing settlement and stated the total amount paid for the previous year. His faith was such that he stood ready to pay the same amount all over again if the Lord's servants needed it for the work." (*Conference Report,* April 1966, p. 52.)

The primary responsibilities of the Church as the custodian of the fulness of the gospel are threefold: (1) to preach the gospel, (2) to perfect the lives of the individual members, and (3) to make it possible for members to save their dead by vicarious service in the temple. Vast sums of money are required to effectively carry out these responsibilities. Inasmuch as these programs are also the responsibility of each member of the Church, the need to support them constitutes the major obligation of each one, and tithing is the principal source of income in achieving this end. Since tithing is used to support the missionary system, to help members perfect their own lives and assist others in perfecting theirs, and to provide the means for the work of salvation for the dead, we can understand why the payment of it is a major contribution to these ends.

In all of these areas there is direct participation in other ways than tithing. Latter-day Saints know that their full participation is the sure way to salvation here and in eternal worlds. They remember these words of the Lord: "Therefore, let your hearts be comforted; for all things shall work together for good to them that walk uprightly, and to the sanctification of the church." (D&C 100:15.)

Toward the end of the last century, President Joseph F. Smith related the following story of a faithful member who, through his observing this "practical religion," was blessed bounteously: "A short time ago I met a brother—I need not call his name, for he is but one among thousands who can bear the same testimony, not only by the word of mouth but by the evidences of thrift, of prosperity, of progress and of improvement which surround him in the midst of the deserts. This season he has gathered in rich harvests, his farms having produced in abundance, while the farms of many of his neighbors are clogged with weeds, and their harvests have been only one-half or one-third what his has been. How do you account for it? I account for it in the fact that God has

4   blessed him; and so does he, for he is an intelligent man, a man that not only labors wisely and prudently, but in the fear of God, and in the desire of his heart to obey his laws. He said to me and my companion with whom we were traveling: 'God has blessed me because I have striven to keep his laws, and because I have been true to my family.' He went out there upon the desert seven or eight years ago, impoverished by persecution and exile, being driven from his home and from his affairs, compelled to wander in exile for years, part of the time preaching the gospel. He returned seven or eight years ago, and settled down upon the desert. Today, out of the earth, the burning sands, he has produced beautiful homes, he has fruitful fields, which are spread out before the eyes of any man who wishes to go and look upon them. He pays his tithing, he remembers his offerings, he is obedient to the laws of God, and he is not afraid to bear testimony to his friends and neighbors that it is through obedience that God has blessed and prospered him, and made him what he is today. He is not the only one; there are others who are prospered in like manner. And I testify that it is because God has blessed him, and his soil, and his labors, that he obtained the increase, and secured the blessings for which he sought and labored. He has acted in good faith with the Lord; the Lord has known his heart, and has blessed him accordingly, and he is prosperous today in that desert, while as to many of his neighbors—go and look for yourselves at their broad acres. They tell the story for themselves. His lands are clear from noxious weeds, because he has labored, and taken care of his lands, and because God has inspired him, and enlightened his mind. The Lord has blessed him in his basket and in his store, in his labors and in the thoughts of his mind, he has been inspired and enabled to accomplish the work that he has done: I testify that it is because of man's faith in the promise of the Lord, and his desire to obey his laws, that he is blessed and prospered of him." (*Gospel Doctrine*, pp. 227-28.)

    The history of the Church is replete with examples of converts who were blessed materially as well as spiritually when they lived the principles of the gospel. In 1899 President George Q. Cannon told how the gospel had improved the lives of converts in various lands.Often poverty, deprivation, and drudgery were their lot, but when they accepted the fulness of the gospel, great changes were effected in their lives. He told of one such case:

"... I heard one man say . . . that in Scandinavia, where he lived, he envied the position of the horse, and wished he had been born a horse. Why? Because the horse was cared for; the horse was fed; the horse was carefully housed; he had value; when he died it was a loss to his master; but as to him, the working man, he might die, and what loss would it be to anybody? Not to his master. It might be to his wife, or to his children, but not to his master. He could toil, could go hungry; he could go partly clad; he could go miserably housed and provided for; the animal that possessed value was worth something; that could be cared for, carefully blanketed at night, fed well and kept in a warm stable, and if he were sick taken care of that he might not die. This man's statements concerning his feelings were very strongly put; but his condition was that of thousands when this Gospel reached them. What has it done for them? It has lifted them up; it has made them feel that they are the children of God—peers of every one else on the earth, no matter how rich, no matter how learned, no matter how many advantages others may possess, they are equal before the Lord with all of them. 'Mormonism' has done this for the world. It has made every man, that is worthy, a Priest of God; it has had this effect. . . . Every man that has embraced this Gospel is raised to this dignity and to this power." (*Conference Report*, April 1899, pp. 18-19.)

Why do Latter-day Saints pay tithing? There are many reasons, based upon the individual's own experiences as well as those of other members of the Church. It is possible that some today may be in the dire circumstances described in the foregoing example. Nonetheless, when gospel covenants are lived, the blessings of the Lord are received.

Through paying tithing, we receive increased wisdom in meeting the financial needs of life. A common experience, attested by many faithful tithe payers, is that after one-tenth of one's income has been paid to the Lord, the remaining nine-tenths goes as far in meeting obligations as did the whole. The economies effected in living other gospel principles also make it possible for us to live this important law. For those who have used tobacco, tea, coffee, and alcoholic beverages, it has been found that the cost of these harmful substances often equals the amount paid as tithing.

Adherence to the principles of truth—including payment of an honest tithe—requires self-discipline. When we receive the

6 Holy Ghost by the laying on of hands by an authorized servant of the Lord, many blessings are brought into our lives—and probably the greatest factor in self-discipline is the influence of the Holy Ghost. Further motivation and determination to discipline one's life come from the Latter-day Saint philosophy of life—a knowledge of the life before this, the purpose of mortality, and the promises of eternal rewards in the future life.

President George Albert Smith gave this advice concerning the payment of tithing: "The Lord has given us the privilege of contributing one-tenth of our interest, for His Church, for the development of His work in the world. Those who pay their tithing receive their blessing. If we do not desire the blessing, we may withhold our contribution. The Lord promises His blessing if we honor His law and not otherwise." (*Conference Report*, April 1941, p. 25.)

2

THE HISTORY
OF TITHING

"The law of tithing is of very ancient origin. How early it was observed by the people of God is not clearly set forth in the Scriptures, but we have an account of its observance as early as the days of Abraham and Melchizedec. We have also, anterior to that, an account given us in the Scriptures of the bringing forward of offerings by Cain and Abel, one bringing the first fruits of the earth, and the other the first fruits of his flocks, as offerings unto the Lord their God." (George Q. Cannon, *Journal of Discourses*, 15:145.)

In the beginning offerings were made to the Lord under the law of sacrifice commanded of Adam. (Moses 5:5-6.) This law demonstrates an important truth regarding man's obligation to the Lord. The Lord did not need the offerings, but man needed to show the Lord that he served him. It was then, as it is today, a test of faith.

The first account of tithing mentioned in the Bible is when Abraham paid one-tenth of all he possessed to Melchizedek, a high priest and king of Salem (Jerusalem). (Genesis 14:18-20; Hebrews 7:1-2.) In a discourse on priesthood the Book of Mormon prophet Alma called upon his people to be humble and, through their repentance, receive the Lord's blessings. He also mentioned the paying of tithes by Abraham: ". . . yea, even our father Abraham paid tithes of one-tenth part of all he possessed." (Alma 13:15.)

The Lord promised Jacob, son of Isaac, in his dream of the ladder ascending into heaven that he would receive the same blessings of prosperity and seed given to his father and Abraham, whereupon Jacob covenanted that he would give a tenth to the Lord. (Genesis 28:10-22.)

In another scripture we learn that all of ancient Israel's possessions were tithed: "And all the tithe of the land, whether of the seed of the land, or of the fruit of the tree, it is the Lord's: it is holy unto the Lord. . . . And concerning the tithe of the herd, or of the flock, even of whatsoever passeth under the rod, the tenth

8   shall be holy unto the Lord." (Leviticus 27:30, 32.) The fruit of the vine and olive yard was converted into wine and oil before the tenth of it was taken. All of this tithe was to be given to the Levites for their inheritance, inasmuch as they did not receive a landed inheritance among the tribes of Israel— "for their service which they serve, even the service of the tabernacle of the congregation." It was expected, however, that they would pay a tenth of what they received. (See Numbers 18:24-27.) The tithe was given to the Levites and other dependent persons every third year. (Deuteronomy 26:12-15.)

In times of religious decline among the Israelites, tithe paying was neglected and a lack of prosperity followed. On the other hand, the people were blessed when they kept the commandments of the Lord. Hezekiah called upon them to pay their tithes, and the response was so good that he had to prepare chambers in the temple precincts for storing the tithes. (2 Chronicles 31:11-12.) In the time of Malachi also, the people were reprimanded for nonpayment of tithes. (Malachi 3:7-10.)

The law of tithing practiced in Old Testament times was an offering for sacred purposes and not a tax. Some nations, however, practiced a tithe. The Lydians offered a tithe of the spoils of war, and the Phoenicians and Carthaginians sent a tithe annually to the Tyrian Hercules. Some of these tithes were occasional payments, some voluntary, and others were required by law. The Egyptians, for example, were required to pay one-fifth of their crops to the Pharaoh. (Genesis 47:24.) (*The New Westminster Dictionary of the Bible,* p. 952.)

The law of tithing continued into the time of Jesus. Because the scribes and Pharisees of his day omitted the "weightier matters of the law" but paid tithe of mint and anise and cummin, they were condemned by Jesus. Significantly, because they had neglected mercy and faith, he said: ". . . these ought ye to have done, and not to leave the other undone." (Matthew 23:23.)

Two methods of financially sustaining The Church of Jesus Christ of Latter-day Saints were revealed in the first decade of its existence. The law of consecration, sometimes referred to as the United Order, was revealed in 1831 as the celestial law by which the economic level of the poor would be raised and the rich would be reduced. (D&C 42:30-42.) The second method was the law of tithing, given in 1838. (D&C 119.)

The Lord gives to his people the law that is suited to the times in which they live. All of his laws are eternal, but not all of them are practiced at the same time. As his people develop the capacity to live greater laws, they receive them. Sometimes a law may be given to test faith. It is probable that this was one reason why the law of consecration was revealed in our dispensation. The immediate purpose was to care for the poor. The Prophet Joseph Smith was told that he "should go to the Ohio," where the law governing this matter would be given to him. (D&C 38:32.)

The law of consecration, together with other gospel laws, was then revealed for the economic and spiritual welfare of the Saints. It gave the participant an opportunity to satisfy his economic wants, provide for his children, and help others to receive the same blessings. This cooperative plan, revealed in Doctrine and Covenants 42, verses 29-39, provided that the consecrator legally surrender his properties, for which he received a stewardship by legal deed. From the use of this stewardship he would maintain his family and provide a surplus, which would be used for the good of the community. A person's free agency would be respected not only in his entering the system but also if he chose to leave it. All members of the Church would be taken care of provided they were diligent in keeping their covenants. Provision was made for the welfare of widows and orphans. (D&C 83:1-6.) This order gave opportunity for the members to progress spiritually through uprooting selfishness and greed and increasing their ability to subordinate self for the common good. The ultimate end of this program was to make the Church independent from all the creatures on the earth. (D&C 78:13-14.)

Several reasons may be given for discontinuing the law of consecration in 1834. Persecution of the Church in Missouri shortened the time when this law was operative. The members gathering there had either sold their possessions or given them away, leaving little to consecrate. (*History of the Church,* 1:381.) Also, the Lord revealed that due to their weaknesses the Saints did not measure up to the standards necessary to live the law. (D&C 101:6-8; 105:2-6.)

There were times previously when the greater law of consecration was practiced and a virtual Zion existed on the earth. Before Abraham paid tithes to Melchizedek, Enoch was given this socioeconomic order, and his people's oneness of heart and mind in living the law resulted in the elimination of poverty. (Moses 7:18.) The second experience of this kind was that of the Nephites after the Savior's visit to them following his resurrection. Their blessings are described in these verses: ". . . there were no contentions and disputations among them, and every man did deal justly one with another. And they had all things common among them; therefore there were not rich and poor, bond and free, but they were all made free, and partakers of the heavenly gift." (4 Nephi 2-3.)

Tithing is considered a lesser law than the law of consecration, and one of its purposes is to prepare the Saints to live the greater law. (Lorenzo Snow, *Journal of Discourses*, 19:345.) Probably the first time a covenant of tithing was made in our day was when Joseph Smith and Oliver Cowdery covenanted with the Lord that if they had sufficient to pay their debts, they would "give a tenth to be bestowed upon the poor in His Church, or as He shall command." (*History of the Church*, 2:175.) In their prayer regarding this covenant they referred to Jacob, who also sought the blessings of "bread to eat, and raiment to put on" as an example of their own wishes. (Ibid.)

While at Far West, Missouri, on July 8, 1838, the Lord answered the Prophet Joseph Smith's question, "O Lord, show unto thy servants how much thou requirest of the properties of thy people for a tithing." The answer is section 119 of the Doctrine and Covenants.

"Verily, thus saith the Lord, I require all their surplus property to be put into the hands of the bishop of my church in Zion,

"For the building of mine house, and for the laying of the foundation of Zion and for the priesthood, and for the debts of the Presidency of my Church.

"And this shall be the beginning of the tithing of my people.

"And after that, those who have thus been tithed shall pay one-tenth of all their interest annually; and this shall be a standing law unto them forever, for my holy priesthood, saith the Lord.

"Verily I say unto you, it shall come to pass that all those who gather unto the land of Zion shall be tithed of their surplus properties, and shall observe this law, or they shall not be found worthy to abide among you.

"And I say unto you, if my people observe not this law, to keep it holy, and by this law sanctify the land of Zion unto me, that my statutes and my judgments may be kept thereon, that it may be most holy, behold, verily I say unto you, it shall not be a land of Zion unto you.

"And this shall be an ensample unto all the stakes of Zion. Even so. Amen."

President Joseph F. Smith believed that the greater law of consecration "comprehended larger things, greater power, and a more speedy accomplishment of the purposes of the Lord." Since the people were unprepared to live it, the law of tithing was revealed in order that there might be the means of "gathering of the poor, for the spreading of the gospel to the nations of the earth, for the maintenance of those who were required to give their constant attention, day in and day out, to the work of the Lord." (*Gospel Doctrine*, p. 225.)

Throughout this dispensation the leaders of the Church have admonished the Saints to pay their tithing. Following the martyrdom of the Prophet Joseph Smith and his brother Hyrum, the Council of the Twelve, under the leadership of Brigham Young, issued an epistle in which they reiterated this principle as binding upon all the Saints. (*History of the Church*, 7:358.) Although the revelation had been given and the leaders had taught the need to comply with the law of tithing, full compliance was not forthcoming. Tithing may or may not have been one of the requirements to receive a temple recommend before 1881; in that year Wilford Woodruff, President of the Council of the Twelve, confirmed President John Taylor's decision that the payment of tithing was a requisite to go to the temple. (*Journal of Discourses*, 22:207-8.)

Upon the death of President Woodruff in 1898, Lorenzo Snow, then eighty-five years old, became President of the Church. Grave financial conditions existed in the Church due to harassment by the United States government regarding plural marriage, which resulted in expensive litigation over Church property, and "the difficulties which had to be contended with during the protracted persecutions under the laws of Congress and the peculiar constructions of the Courts in their enforcements and other circumstances of an adverse nature." (Thomas C. Romney, *The Life of Lorenzo Snow*, Salt Lake City, *Deseret News*, 1955, p. 451.) Over the years the Church had had to borrow money and had not been able to pay the interest on its indebtedness. The issuance of bonds helped alleviate the immediate condition, but the Church was still in need of becoming financially sound. President Snow referred to this condition as the "bottomless pit" and "the unfathomable deep," and sought divine guidance to this financial problem.

The following information is taken from articles written by LeRoi Snow, son of and private secretary to President Snow, who was a witness to the events that in a few years brought the Church out of financial bondage. He wrote the following concerning events that took place in May 1899:

"During the night, in the Bee Hive House, the Lord instructed my father to go to St. George, but did not tell him the purpose of the trip. I was the first in his bedroom that morning and I shall never forget his glorious appearance as I saw him sitting upright in his bed. His face was almost white and his eyes shone as I had never seen them before. All he said was: 'I am going to St. George.' These were his first words at the breakfast table and again on entering his office. Preparations were hurriedly made." (LeRoi C. Snow, "From Despair to Freedom Through Tithing," *Church News*, March 29, 1941, p. 6.)

The party of seventeen left Salt Lake City on May 15, 1899, by railroad for the southern Utah community of St. George, traveling the final seventy miles in horse-drawn carriages. As they came closer to their destination, they saw the effects of the worst drought in thirty-five years. The streams had dried up, thousands of cattle were dying on the ranges, crops were drying up, and frosts had taken toll of the grape crop. The people were discouraged. Some of them had moved away and many who remained were not willing to risk planting seeds because of the drought. Amid these conditions President Snow was perplexed as to the reason why the Lord had instructed him to make this trip and to take so many of the General Authorities when other matters could have occupied their time.

On Wednesday, May 17, the special conference convened in the St. George Tabernacle. This report was written of what occurred:

". . . It was during one of these meetings that President Snow received the renewed revelation on tithing. I was sitting at a table on the stand, reporting the proceedings, when all at once father paused in his discourse. Complete stillness filled the room. I shall never forget the thrill as long as I live. When he commenced to speak again his voice strengthened and the inspiration of God seemed to come over him, as well as over the entire assembly. His eyes seemed to brighten and his countenance to shine. He was filled with unusual power. Then he revealed to the Latter-day Saints the vision that was before him.

"God manifested to him there and then not only the purpose of the call to visit the Saints in the South, but also Lorenzo Snow's special mission, the great work for which God had prepared and preserved him, and he unveiled the vision to the people. He told them that he could see, as he had never realized before, how the law of tithing had been neglected by the people, also that the Saints, themselves, were heavily in debt, as well as the Church, and now through strict obedience to this law—the paying of a full and honest tithing—not only would the Church be relieved of its great indebtedness, but through the blessings of the Lord this would also be the means of freeing the Latter-day Saints from their individual obligations, and they would become a prosperous people.

"Directly on tithing, President Snow said:

" 'The word of the Lord is: The time has now come for every Latter-day Saint, who calculates to be prepared for the future and to hold his feet strong upon a proper foundation, to do the will of the Lord and to pay his tithing in full. That is the word of the Lord to you, and it will be the word of the Lord to every settlement throughout the land of Zion.' " (LeRoi S. Snow, "The Lord's Way Out of Bondage," *Improvement Era*, July 1938, p. 439.)

Despite the drought conditions, President Snow promised the Saints that if they would pay a full tithing and plant their crops, rains would come to drench the land, and they would reap a bounteous harvest.

On the return journey to Salt Lake City, he taught the law of tithing in sixteen settlements. Regarding one of these memorable meetings, his son wrote: "When the returning party reached Nephi, where we were to take train for home, President Snow called the members all together in a meeting which will never be forgotten by those who were present. He commissioned every one present to be his special witness to the fact that the Lord had given this revelation to him. He put all the party under covenant and promise not only to obey the law of tithing themselves but also that each would bear witness to this special manifestation and

14   would spread the tithing message at every opportunity. He made wonderful promises to those who would be faithful to these admonitions." (Ibid., p. 440.)

Upon President Snow's return to Church headquarters, a campaign was instituted to instruct members in the law of tithing.

These were troubled days for President Snow, as he read the daily weather reports from the St. George area. Week after week the rains did not come. His son wrote that one day he approached his father's bedroom and heard him talking. In looking through the open door he saw President Snow on his knees pouring out his heart to the Lord: "Oh, Lord, why didst thou make those promises to the good people in St. George, if they are not to be fulfilled? Thou didst promise them, if they would accept thy command to obey the law of tithing, thou wouldst send the rains from heaven and bless them with a bounteous harvest. These good people accepted thy word and are not only paying a tenth of their income, but they are offering all they have to thee. Do keep thy promise and vindicate the words of thy servant through whom thou didst speak." (Ibid., p. 440.)

Several days later, on August 2, word came that rain had fallen in the St. George area, drenching the ground and filling the streams. For two months the Saints had complied with the law of tithing, and they had planted crops; now the Lord's promises began to be fulfilled. Although President Snow did not live to see the Church free of financial bondage, his successor, Joseph F. Smith, reported to the Saints on April 5, 1907:

"The tithes of the people during the year 1906 have surpassed the tithes of any other year. . . . I want to say another thing to you, and I do so by way of congratulations, and that is, that we have, by the blessings of the Lord and the faithfulness of the Saints in paying their tithing, been able to pay off our bonded indebtedness. Today the Church of Jesus Christ of Latter-day Saints owes not a dollar that it cannot pay at once. At last we are in a position that we can pay as we go. We do not have to borrow any more, and will not have to if the Latter-day Saints continue to live their religion and observe this law of tithing. It is the law of revenue to the Church." (Ibid., pp. 441-42.)

The following statement from President Snow is as applicable today as when spoken at the end of the last century: "Well, the Latter-day Saints are a good people and the Lord loves us. He loves us because we are His sons and daughters. Because He loves us He has forgiven us our forgetfulness of this holy law in the past. . . . He will not forgive this people any longer should we continue this dilatory way of paying tithing." ("From Despair to Freedom Through Tithing," *op. cit.*, p. 8.)

3
WHAT IS TITHING?

"I like to think of the Lord as a partner, because the essence of partnership is a sharing of profits. It is however indispensable in a partnership that there shall also be a sharing of the burdens of the enterprise. The honor and the satisfaction that come to one in realization that he lives his life in partnership with God is to me a lofty and exalting thought. One cannot hope to realize the profits from that venture without bearing his portion of the expense—the giving which is requisite." (Stephen L Richards, *Conference Report*, April 1929, p. 51.)

The revelation on tithing in the Doctrine and Covenants defines it as "one-tenth of all their interest annually." (D&C 119:4.) Interest means increase, income, profit, compensation. There are some who consider a tithe to be less than one-tenth. Concerning this President Stephen L Richards said: "Tithing does not mean one-fiftieth, nor one-thirtieth, nor one-twentieth. Tithing means one-tenth. I have sometimes wondered what a part tithing means. I have never seen any definition of it, but I know what a tithing means. So far as I know, there is only one tithing, and that is one-tenth." (*Conference Report*, April 1952, p. 84.)

While a tithe is one-tenth of one's income, the computation of one's income can differ depending upon how he obtains the income. The Lord expects each person to be honest with him. Consequently, each person must determine whether his tithing is an honest one. President Joseph F. Smith said: "Now, you are at liberty to do as you please in regard to this matter. You can choose which ever course you wish. But let me say to you that as we measure out so will it be measured back unto us again. When we go to dickering with the Lord, probably He will dicker with us; and if He undertakes to do so, we shall get the worst of it." (*Conference Report*, April 1899, p. 69.)

Inasmuch as tithe is based on one's interest, or income, the calculation of the income is different for the self-employed than for the person who works for someone else. The income of the businessman, the farmer, or any other self-employed person is the

profit he derives from his enterprise; in other words, the profit he
derives after deducting the expenses required to make the profit is
his income.

What is to be tithed of the salaried person's income, the gross
or take-home pay? This question is frequently raised today because
more often than not, taxes are deducted from the wage earner's
salary. If the worker were to receive his gross income without taxes
deducted, it might be easier to understand what income should be
tithed. When he was serving as Presiding Bishop of the Church,
Elder LeGrand Richards addressed himself to the numerous questions raised regarding what constitutes a tithe. "We have many
inquiries at our office, constantly, about the matter of deducting
taxes, income taxes, etc., before paying tithing," he said, "and we
are told that in some cases the Saints are advised to do this, by
their bishops. I think the bishops are being pretty liberal with the
Lord's money. Taxes are no different from what they have always
been except in amount and manner of payment. We have never
expected to pay our taxes out of the Lord's tenth." (*Conference
Report*, April 1944, p. 45.)

Questions have also been raised by those whose income is
made in their own businesses. Elder Richards related the following
experience: "For some time I have felt that some farmers do not
figure their tithing the way I think it should be figured. One good
farmer said to me, 'Bishop, I know just how to figure my tithing. I
have a jar in my kitchen cabinet and every time I sell anything I
put a tenth of it in the jar, then I pay it for tithing.' I said, 'Is that
all you pay?' He said, 'Yes, isn't that enough?' 'Well,' I said, 'your
brother who lives up here a few miles earns a hundred dollars a
month and pays ten dollars tithing; he buys his groceries, his milk,
his meat, and his eggs with the money he has left after paying his
tithing. Should a farmer not figure his tithing on all he consumes
and his surplus and the gain of his land?' " (Ibid.)

Elder James E. Talmage pointed out that the recording angels
have a better system of bookkeeping than ours. Tithing is not the
amount of money one pays to the Lord, but whether the payment
is an honest tenth. "The one who pays with honest heart the ten
cent tithe," he said, "if it be a true tithe, will rank higher on those
books than the one who pays a thousand dollars when that is only a
tenth of a tithe for him. . . .

"When you are in doubt as to just how you should calculate

18   your tithes, reverse the terms as we sometimes do in solving complex mathematical problems, and suppose for the time being that the Lord has said this; let us postulate this as an assumed law given to the Church: 'In order to show my love for my people, the faithful members of my Church, it is my will, saith the Lord, that each one shall receive from my storehouse, the storehouse of my church, at regular intervals during the year, an amount equal to one-tenth of his income.' Now my dear brother, sit down and calculate how much the Lord owes you under that kind of law, and then go pay it to your bishop." (*Conference Report*, October 1928.)

Tithing in The Church of Jesus Christ of Latter-day Saints is voluntary, unlike a tax that is required by law with penalties exacted if the tax is not paid. There was a time when the enemies of the Church falsely charged that "the 'Mormon' people are compelled to pay tithing, that the authorities of the Church demand it of them, that it is made obligatory upon them, and is tyrannically exacted from them all the time. . . . The observance of the law of tithing is voluntary. I can pay my tithing or not, as I choose." (Joseph F. Smith, *Gospel Doctrine*, p. 232.) The following statements from President Brigham Young are examples of the policy of the Church regarding tithing: "We do not ask anybody to pay Tithing, unless they are disposed to do so; but if you pretend to pay Tithing, pay it like honest men." (*Journal of Discourses* 8:202.) "The people are not compelled to pay their tithing, they do as they please about it, it is urged upon them only as a matter of duty between them and their God." (Ibid., 12:36.)

When the payment of tithing is voluntary, does it follow that it is not required? The living of every principle of the gospel is a requirement if we are to receive the blessings of those principles in this life and eventual exaltation in the celestial kingdom. The word of the Lord is this: "And no man receiveth a fulness unless he keepeth his commandments. He that keepeth his commandments receiveth truth and light, until he is glorified in truth and knoweth all things." (D&C 93:27-28.)

Elder James E. Talmage stated: "There is an important distinction between tithes and other offerings. While the observance of the tithing law must be willing and voluntary, tithe-paying is nevertheless required, demanded in fact, by the Lord of those who, by their own free will, have become His covenant children by baptism." (*The Articles of Faith*, p. 527.)

President Joseph F. Smith taught that our faithfulness would be known by observance of the law of tithing. (*Gospel Doctrine*, p. 227.) In this respect it is as essential as baptism for the remission of sins or any salvation principle of the gospel.

Sometimes a voluntary offering to the Lord may be thought of as a gift rather than required for salvation. From the foregoing discussion it should be apparent that tithing is a debt rather than a gift. Elder Howard W. Hunter of the Council of the Twelve pointed out that there is a substantial difference between a gift and a debt: "A gift is a voluntary transfer of money or property without consideration. . . . No one owes the obligation to make a gift. If tithing is a gift, we could give whatever we please, when we please, or make no gift at all. It would place our Heavenly Father in the very same category as the street beggar to whom we might toss a coin in passing. The Lord has established the law of tithing, and because it is his law, it becomes our obligation to observe it if we love him and have a desire to keep his commandments and receive his blessings. In this way it becomes a debt." (*Conference Report*, April 1964, p. 35.)

Because tithing is a debt, we can understand why the prophet Malachi charged Israel with robbing God by withholding its tithes and offerings. (Malachi 3:8-9.)

In the early days of the restored church, when the law of consecration was in effect, all property was placed in the hands of the bishop and a stewardship given in return to the consecrator. When a surplus resulted from the stewardship, it was also consecrated to the Church to be used for temple building, for the priesthood, and for the debts of the Presidency of the Church. (D&C 119:2.) In addition, consecrations kept in the storehouse were for the support of widows, orphans, and the poor, and to provide stewardships for children whose parents were unable to give them stewardships. (D&C 83:1-6.)

Later the law of tithing became the source of revenue for the Lord's church. Under the law of tithing, the responsibility for those in need was still that of the individual as far as possible, and then the Church would assist. The Lord provided under that law that when a person came into the Church he should give his surplus property first and then a tithe annually. Franklin D. Richards, Church Historian, said that surplus property in the revelation is that which remains after a necessary subsistence is enjoyed. "Is not the first and most necessary use of a man's property that he feed, clothe and provide a home for himself and family?" (*Journal of Discourses* 23:313.) This definition of surplus property was known to the Church leaders from the time the revelation on tithing was given.

There came a time when it was felt that this provision of the law of tithing was not to be in force, according to President Joseph Fielding Smith: "In more recent times the Church has not called upon the members to give all their surplus property to the Church, but it has been the requirement according to the covenant, that they pay the tenth." (*Church History and Modern Revelation*, Deseret Book Co., 1953, 2:92.)

Although it is not a part of the law of tithing, members of the Church still have an opportunity to contribute part of their surplus means for purposes other than the uses to which tithing is put. These contributions are for fast offerings, building funds, stake and ward budgets, and other purposes.

How well we live the commandments of the Lord is determined in a large measure by our conscience, or knowledge of right and wrong, with the compulsion to do right. One purpose of the gospel is to help us perfect our lives. "Men are, that they might have joy," said a Nephite prophet. (2 Nephi 2:25.) Joy comes by observance of the laws of God when the living of these laws becomes so ingrained in our consciousness that the conscience rejects anything less than full compliance with the teachings of the Spirit. When the General Authorities say that we are to live a law of the gospel, such as tithing, in accordance with our consciences, they are saying that our eternal blessings will be determined by how well our consciences are in agreement with the principles of the gospel. Those who pay less than one-tenth of their income as tithing may find interest in the following story related by President Heber J. Grant:

"On the subject of tithing I heard a very splendid illustration given by a teacher in one of our children's classes: She brought with her ten beautiful red apples. She explained that everything we have in the world came to us from the Lord, and she said, 'Now, if I give one of you these ten apples, will you give me one of them back again? Now, any one of you children that will do that, hold up your hand.'

"Of course, they all held up their hands. Then she said, 'That is what the Lord does for us. He gives us the ten apples, but he requests that we return one to him to show our appreciation of that gift.'

"The trouble with some people is that when they get the ten apples, they eat up nine of them, and then they cut the other in two and give the Lord half of what is left. Some of them cut the apple in two and eat up one-half of it and then hold up the other half and ask the Lord to take a bite. That is about as near as they see fit to share properly and show their gratitude to the Lord." (*Conference Report*, April 1945, pp. 5-6.)

Will the true Latter-day Saint do anything less than pay a full tithing?

4

ATTITUDES TOWARD TITHING

"For as he thinketh in his heart, so is he." (Proverbs 23:7.) Our attitudes or opinions determine what we do about a principle of the gospel. Our beliefs about tithing are often molded by a lack of true knowledge or a lack of conviction that blessings will follow obedience. Often the person of weak faith rationalizes the commandment to pay one-tenth of his income to the Lord through His church. Many and varied are the reasons given by such a person, who does not recognize that success in this life and in the eternal worlds requires full compliance to the commandments.

Excuses are easy to make in an effort to quiet our consciences. However, this practice does not give the desired effect to those who have strong faith in the Lord, for the sharp conscience will not sustain the rationalization of gospel principles. Let us first turn our attention to the attitude of the faithful Latter-day Saint.

A fundamental truth of the gospel is expressed in these words: "For of him unto whom much is given much is required; and he who sins against the greater light shall receive the greater condemnation." (D&C 82:3.)

Tithing is the Lord's method of promoting and sustaining his work upon the earth. However, in an ultimate sense tithing does not make him richer, for the fulness of the earth is his. By his power he could bring forth the treasures of the earth for his purposes, but this kind of generosity would defeat a fundamental purpose for man—that he might prove himself by doing all things whatsoever the Lord would command him. (Abraham 3:25.) Tithing is a generous way of sustaining the Lord's work. He asks our obedience to a principle that requires one-tenth of our income in return for the opportunity of an earth life with its attendant blessings.

President John Taylor took this point of view regarding the payment of tithing: "The Lord does not care a straw whether we pay our Tithing or not, it does not make Him one particle richer or poorer, the gold and silver are his and the cattle upon a thousand hills, the world and all its fulness belong to him for he organized and framed it; but as it is of what benefit is it to him. He wants in the first place to get men to acknowledge God, I was going to say in one little carnal principle, one little earthly principle, he wants to get them to acknowledge him, by giving him a certain little part, or one-tenth of what he gives to them to see whether they will be honest in this trifle, to see whether they will act as honorable high-minded men or not, or whether they will try to cheat him out of it. If we do this honestly and conscientiously until we have fulfilled our duty, we are then prepared for anything else. It is the principle and not the Tithing we pay that is esteemed of the Lord, he cares not for our Tithing but he cares about our doing right. If we cannot be faithful in a few things, we cannot expect to be made rulers over many things." (*Journal of Discourses,* 10:281.)

Elder George Q. Morris expressed the Lord's generosity in a different way: "The singular thing is that he has arranged that he must give $10,000 to get $1,000 back for his work. That may seem a very odd way of doing it, but that is his generous method; and the only way the Lord can get $1,000 contributed to the carrying on of his work under the tithing system is to give $10,000. I will leave it for you to figure out to whom he is going to give $10,000, whether it will be to those who keep it all, or whether it will be to those who turn back the $1,000 that he requires for his work. If we will pay our honest tithing to God, he will bless us and prosper us and increase our faith, and I believe the Lord has a lot of things to do that he can only do through people who have faith to pay their honest tithing." (*Conference Report,* April 1953, p. 112.)

Implicit faith in the Lord's commandments is notably illustrated in the scriptures in such instances as Abraham's obedience to the Lord's commandment to offer up his son Isaac (Genesis 22:1-13) and in Adam's obedience in the offering of sacrifices: "And after many days an angel of the Lord appeared unto Adam, saying: Why dost thou offer sacrifices unto the Lord? And Adam said unto him: I know not, save the Lord commanded me." (Moses 5:6.)

This obedience by the father of the human race illustrates well the important principle that those who have genuine faith in the Lord will follow his commandments, though the reason for doing so may not be readily apparent. Another truth is illustrated in the angel's reply: "And then the angel spake, saying: This thing is a similitude of the sacrifice of the Only Begotten of the Father,

24 which is full of grace and truth. Wherefore, thou shalt do all that thou doest in the name of the Son, and thou shalt repent and call upon God in the name of the Son forevermore." (Moses 5:7-8.)

Because of Adam's faithfulness to the commandment without knowing the reason, blessings of unusual magnitude followed: "And in that day the Holy Ghost fell upon Adam, which beareth record of the Father and the Son, saying: I am the Only Begotten of the Father from the beginning, henceforth and forever, that as thou hast fallen thou mayest be redeemed, and all mankind, even as many as will." (Moses 5:9.)

In blessed exultation, Adam and Eve rejoiced in the contemplation of the privilege of earth life, though it was necessary for them to live amid conditions of good and evil and to be obedient in order that they might have joy in this life and eternal life in the world to come. (Moses 5:10-11.) The angel taught the important lesson that redemption from sin comes from the Only Begotten Son of God in whose name they were to serve. Furthermore, "even as many as will" may be redeemed, by sincere faith in the Father, though the reasons for his commandments may not be known immediately. This faith will bring the greatest of blessings of eternal life, exaltation in the celestial kingdom. (D&C 76:54-70.)

In drawing a lesson from the experience of Adam, President Spencer W. Kimball said: "Had Adam waited until he could have fully understood and rationalized the program, perhaps in the meantime his family would have fallen away from the truth, and he himself might have lost his faith. He needed something tangible—a constant sacrifice—to help him to remember the coming of the Savior at a later time. And so we partake of the sacrament to remind us of the sacrifice that the Savior did make, and now we may pay our tithes which will be a constant reminder to us of the promises and the requirements of our Heavenly Father. So each time we pay our tithes it is a personal sacrifice and brings with it a blessing in faith and closeness to our Heavenly Father." (*Conference Report,* October 1951, p. 85.)

Individuals of weak faith may draw upon a number of excuses for not paying tithing. Probably the most common excuse is that the money on hand is not sufficient to pay tithing. "I can't afford it. My household expenses and other demands made upon me for finances are too great." Many are the answers to this claim. The faithful Latter-day Saint believes that, in essence, he is paying his tithing with faith and not money. When it is claimed by some that they cannot afford to pay tithing, Elder George Q. Morris said, "they should say they haven't faith enough to pay tithing." (*Conference Report,* April 1953, p. 111.)

The Lord has promised through his prophets that he will open the windows of heaven and pour out blessings upon his faithful children. (Malachi 3:10.) Is this promise of no effect? Faith in Christ is the first requisite to the blessings of heaven.

It has always seemed to the author that the person most in need of the Lord's assistance is the one who is in debt and unable of himself to surmount his financial problems. If this individual does not pay his tithing, he is virtually saying, "I don't want to get out of debt." From whom could we receive greater help in working out the solution to our problems than from the Lord? Has he not promised blessings to the obedient? What about the wisdom obtained from the Lord and put into daily action in our being better managers of our finances?

Wise budgeting increases our ability to pay our obligations, including our obligation to the Lord. Many Latter-day Saints testify that obedience to the commandments brings peace of mind, a spiritual blessing, which allows them to utilize and accomplish more with the remaining nine-tenths of their income than if they had not been honest with the Lord. The words of a Nephite prophet come with the stamp of faith and experience: "And now, I say unto you, my brethren, that after ye have known and have been taught all these things, if ye should transgress and go contrary to that which has been spoken, that ye do withdraw yourselves from the Spirit of the Lord, that it may have no place in you to guide you in wisdom's paths that ye may be blessed, prospered, and preserved." (Mosiah 2:36.)

Our discussion on this allegation "I can't afford it" has been primarily on temporal blessings, but what about the spiritual? When someone says to himself, "I can't afford it," isn't he saying, in essence, "I can't afford to receive the joy and happiness that come through obedience, the peace of mind so necessary in a world of turmoil, the help to rear my children as faithful members of the Church, the ultimate blessing of exaltation with my family"? Will his faith permit him to obtain all these blessings, or is it insufficient to bring "forth the blessings of heaven"?

On the other end of the scale is the excuse that with an income

26 sufficient to take care of all our necessities and to have many luxuries, one-tenth is too much to give to the Church. This claim is not always stated, but it lies in the back of the minds of many who paid tithing when their income was relatively smaller but now find it difficult to surrender the larger amount one-tenth would exact from them. Tithing now represents in their minds a new car, substantial luxuries for recreation, and the many other places money may be used to satisfy their desires for pleasure. President Heber J. Grant referred to a member of the Church who paid only about $600 tithing on an income of $45,000 a year; the tithe paid should have been $4,500, still leaving over $40,000 for the man. President Grant commented, "If he had the right vision his heart should almost have burst with gratitude to God for the difference, rather than dwell upon the amount of tithing to be paid." (*Gospel Standards*, p. 65.)

The love of money looms large in the hearts of many when in its place the love of God, given as the first great commandment, should be uppermost. The love of money more than God is demonstrated not only by persons of great wealth but also by members of the Church of modest means who do not pay tithing. Not paying tithing marks a person as devoid of the spirit of the gospel, for he does not labor for the building up of the kingdom of God upon the earth.

Another excuse for not paying tithing is, "I don't owe the Lord anything, because I have worked hard for that which I possess," or, expressed in another way, "My income was received from the use of my mind in my profession, and I do not believe that I owe the Lord anything." A fundamental reason why these persons hold to this attitude is their lack of understanding of the purpose of life. They do not recognize that they are the children of God, born in a premortal world. They have lost the precious knowledge that this earth life is a short span in an everlasting life reaching back into the eons of time before birth and extending into the limitless future. In the eternity of time they will find ample opportunity to reflect upon their actions in this period of mortality, remembering that they made commitments with their Eternal Father and his Son Jesus Christ that they would do all things required of them. This contract was made before we came to earth. It is renewed in the temporal body by baptism and by covenants made in the temple. Do we, as children of God, owe him anything? How well the prophets have emphasized that everything we possess, even life itself, is owed to our Heavenly Father! He created all things—this earth and the means of sustaining life—for our benefit because we are his spirit children. The beautiful twenty-fourth Psalm reads:

"The earth is the Lord's, and the fulness thereof; the world, and they that dwell therein.

"For he hath founded it upon the seas, and established it upon the floods.

"Who shall ascend into the hill of the Lord? or who shall stand in his holy place?

"He that hath clean hands, and a pure heart; who hath not lifted up his soul unto vanity, nor sworn deceitfully.

"He shall receive the blessing from the Lord, and righteousness from the God of his salvation."

Read the words of the wise King Benjamin, who spoke as one who knows the purposes to which the tithe is put:

"For behold, are we not all beggars? Do we not all depend upon the same Being, even God, for all the substance which we have, for both food and raiment, and for gold, and for silver, and for all the riches which we have of every kind?

"And now, if God, who has created you, on whom you are dependent for your lives and for all that ye have and are, doth grant unto you whatsoever ye ask that is right, in faith, believing that ye shall receive, O then, how ye ought to impart of the substance that ye have one to another." (Mosiah 4:19, 21.)

Another excuse given for nonpayment of tithing is that which is given by the person who, when his child is to be married in the temple, asks for a temple recommend from his bishop but refuses to pay tithing because he does not think that one should have to "buy his way into the temple." What has already been said about the debt we owe to the Lord and the other reasons given for paying tithing are also answers to this misconception. Again, a person who makes such a statement does not understand the fundamental first principle of salvation—faith in the Lord Jesus Christ. Among the earmarks of faith are those matters which demonstrate that we truly follow the Master's teachings. An outstanding example of the need to give of one's substance is shown in the Savior's counsel to the rich young ruler who believed he had lived the commandments that give eternal life: "Now when Jesus heard these things, he said unto him, Yet lackest thou one thing: sell all that thou hast, and distribute unto the poor, and thou shalt have treasure in heaven: and come, follow me." (Luke 18:22.)

The Lord does not ask us to give everything away; he requires only that we give one-tenth of our increase and follow him. Normally, the person who believes that his contribution is unnecessary to demonstrate his faith in Christ does not follow the Lord in keeping the other commandments. If he followed the Lord's counsel to be an active agent in the kingdom, he would learn that the way to strong faith is through keeping the commandments, including the law of tithing. (D&C 38:40.) The Prophet Joseph Smith declared: "Let us here observe, that a religion that does not require the sacrifice of all things never has power sufficient to produce the faith necessary unto life and salvation; for, from the first existence of man, the faith necessary unto the enjoyment of life and salvation never could be obtained without the sacrifice of all earthly things." (*Lectures on Faith*, Lecture 6, no. 7.)

Another excuse given for not paying a full tithe is the belief that service rendered in church callings ought to be a sufficient offering to warrant the advantages of church membership. This alibi is based upon an incomplete knowledge of what is involved in working out one's salvation. The shortsightedness of the argument is the inability to distinguish between the temporal advantages of church activity and the spiritual blessings that come from full obedience to the commandments of God. A person who uses such an alibi might be one of those to whom President Spencer W. Kimball referred when he said: "There are many people in this Church today who think they live, but they are dead to the spiritual things. And I believe even many who are making pretenses of being active are also spiritually dead. Their service is much of the letter and less of the spirit." (*Conference Report*, April 1951, p. 105.) The Lord has never promised "all that my Father hath" to those who are only part-timers in obedience to the commandments. (D&C 84:35-38; 18:46.)

Excuses or alibis for not paying tithing are all false teachings inspired by the evil one. President Joseph F. Smith warned Latter-day Saints against falling into the trap of accepting false doctrines disguised as truths of the gospel. He classified those who do so into two groups: "First—The hopelessly ignorant, whose lack of intelligence is due to their indolence and sloth, who make but feeble effort, if indeed any at all, to better themselves by reading and study; those who are afflicted with a dread disease that may develop into an incurable malady—laziness. Second—The proud and self-vaunting ones, who read by the lamp of their own conceit; who interpret by rules of their own contriving; who have become a law unto themselves, and so pose as the sole judges of their own doings. More dangerously ignorant than the first." (*Gospel Doctrine*, p. 373.)

5

SACRIFICE BRINGS FORTH BLESSINGS

"Behold, now it is called today until the coming of the Son of Man, and verily it is a day of sacrifice, and a day for the tithing of my people; for he that is tithed shall not be burned at his coming.

"For after today cometh the burning—this is speaking after the manner of the Lord—for verily I say, tomorrow all the proud and they that do wickedly shall be as stubble; and I will burn them up, for I am the Lord of Hosts; and I will not spare any that remain in Babylon.

"Wherefore, if ye believe me, ye will labor while it is called today." (D&C 64:23-25.)

Giving oneself to the service of the Lord is a requirement for the highest blessings available through the gospel of Jesus Christ. If the offering is consistent with what the Lord requires in terms of time, talents, and means, it is accepted by the Lord. In a sense, what we give to the Lord may be thought of as a sacrifice, and the Lord so expresses it, because it is an individual offering. In some instances the sacrifice may be external giving, such as tithing. An ultimate sacrifice is the contrite heart. The Lord has said: "Verily I say unto you, all among them who know their hearts are honest, and are broken, and their spirits contrite, and are willing to observe their covenants by sacrifice—yea, every sacrifice which I, the Lord, shall command—they are accepted of me." (D&C 97:8.)

To give everything to the Lord is not expected at this time—only when the Lord commands it through his servants. He does require, however, that we give one-tenth of our increase as tithing to his church. In contrast to this small offering is the commandment that, if necessary, we might be called upon to lay down our life for the Lord's sake. Unless we are willing to make that kind of sacrifice, we are not the Lord's disciples. (D&C 103:27-28.) Therefore, if true discipleship demands readiness to lay down our lives, what is our position before the Lord if we fail to pay tithing? Are we the Lord's disciples? The Lord's answer is clear: "He that receiveth my law and doeth it, the same is my disciple; and he that saith he receiveth it and doeth it not, the same is not my disciple, and shall be cast out from among you." (D&C 41:5.)

The prophet Malachi used strong words of accusation against those in his day who were not tithe payers:

"Will a man rob God? Yet ye have robbed me. But ye say, Wherein have we robbed thee? In tithes and offerings.

"Ye are cursed with a curse: for ye have robbed me, even this whole nation.

"Bring ye all the tithes into the storehouse, that there may be meat in mine house, and prove me now herewith, saith the Lord of hosts, if I will not open you the windows of heaven, and pour you out a blessing, that there shall not be room enough to receive it." (Malachi 3:8-10. See also 3 Nephi 24:3-10.)

In reference to Malachi's accusation, Elder Howard W. Hunter of the Council of the Twelve said:

"The words of Malachi in which he accused the people of robbing God bring back to my mind the memories of my class in crimes in law school. Larceny is the unlawful taking and carrying away of things personal with intent to deprive the owner of the same. Embezzlement is defined as the fraudulent appropriation of another's personal property by one to whom it has been entrusted. The distinction between larceny and embezzlement lies in the character of acquiring the possession of the property or money. In larceny there is an unlawful acquisition of the property, while in embezzlement the property which belongs to another is acquired lawfully and then fraudulently converted to the possessor's use.

"In order to memorize these distinctions, I pictured in my mind, to represent larceny, a masked burglar, sneaking about under the cover of darkness, taking that which was not his. To represent the theory of embezzlement I thought of a non-tithepayer. The Lord's share came into his hands lawfully, but he misappropriated it to his own use. This seems to be the accusation of Malachi." (*Conference Report*, April 1964, p. 34.)

President Spencer W. Kimball gave a classic sermon on tithing at general conference in April 1968 in which he discussed a number of cases in which individual members of the Church failed to honor the Lord's commandments regarding tithing. At the conclusion of his sermon, he said:

"Perhaps your attitudes are the product of your misconceptions.

"Would you steal a dollar from your friend? a tire from your neighbor's car? Would you borrow a widow's insurance money with no intent to pay? Do you rob banks? You are shocked at such suggestions. Then, would you rob your God, your Lord, who has made such generous arrangements with you?

"Do you have a right to appropriate the funds of your employer with which to pay your debts, to buy a car, to clothe your family, to feed your children, to build your home?

"Would you take your neighbor's funds to send your children to college, or on a mission? Would you help relatives or friends with funds not your own? Some people get their standards mixed, their ideals out of line. Would you take tithes to pay your building fund, or ward maintenance? Would you supply gifts to the poor with someone else's money? The Lord's money?" (*Conference Report*, April 1968, p. 77.)

The most important reason why we should pay tithing is the one given above: it is a commandment of the Lord. If we do not pay tithing, we are covenant breakers, even to the point of being classified as robbers.

The second major reason for observing the law of tithing is the blessings received for so doing. President Brigham Young, in encouraging the Saints to build the kingdom of God, said:

"Now, you Elders who understand the principles of the kingdom of God, what would you not give, do, or sacrifice, to assist in building up His kingdom upon the earth? Says one, 'I would do anything in my power, anything that the Lord would help me to do, to build up His kingdom.' Says another, 'I would sacrifice all my property.' Wonderful indeed! Do you not know that the possession of your property is like a shadow, or the dew of the morning before the noonday sun, that you cannot have any assurance of its control for a single moment! It is the unseen hand of Providence that controls it. In short, what would you not sacrifice? The Saints sacrifice everything; but, strictly speaking, there is no sacrifice about it. If you give a *penny* for a *million of gold!* a *handful of earth* for a *planet!* a temporary worn out *tenement* for one *glorified,* that will exist, abide, and continue to increase throughout a never ending eternity, what a *sacrifice to be sure!*" (*Journal of Discourses,* 1:114.)

The purpose of all gospel teaching and practice is to prepare people for the blessing of godhood. The Eternal Father, through the sacrifice of his Only Begotten Son, gives a glorified, exalted, resurrected body to the faithful. No blessing in the gospel of Jesus Christ can equal this ultimate of all blessings—to receive "all that my Father hath." (D&C 84:38.)

President Lorenzo Snow once addressed himself to the following words of the apostle Paul: "Let this mind be in you, which was also in Christ Jesus: Who, being in the form of God, thought it not robbery to be equal with God." (Philippians 2:5-6.) President Snow said:

> Hast thou not been unwisely bold,
> Man's destiny to thus unfold?
> To raise, promote such high desire,
> Such vast ambition thus inspire?
> Still, 'tis no phantom that we trace
> Man's ultimatum in life's race;
> This royal path has long been trod
> By righteous men, each now a God:
> As Abra'm, Isaac, Jacob, too,
> First babes, then men—to gods they grew.
> As man now is, our God once was;
> As now God is, so man may be,—
> Which doth unfold man's destiny. . . .
> ("Man's Destiny," *Improvement Era,* June 1919, p. 660.)

Is there really sacrifice of "a penny" or "a handful of earth" for the power of eternal increase throughout a never-ending eternity? What is the power of increase received by the exalted? President Joseph Fielding Smith wrote that it is "the power of eternal increase of posterity. . . . Children born to parents who have obtained, through their faithfulness, the fulness of these blessings, shall be *spirit children* not clothed upon with tabernacles of flesh and bones. *These children will be like we were before we came into this world."* (*Doctrines of Salvation,* Bookcraft, 1955, 2:68-69.)

Teaching that full obedience to the principles of the gospel brings these blessings, President Smith also wrote: "Do you think it would be fair, just, proper, for the Lord to say to us: 'I will give unto you commandments; you may keep them if you will; you may be indifferent about the matter if you will; keep some, reject others; or, partially keep some; and I will punish you, but then I will make it up to you, and all will be well. . . . In other words, *we must receive in our hearts, accept in our hearts every principle of the gospel which has been revealed; and insofar as it is in our power to do so, we must live in accordance with these principles and keep the commandments of God in full."* (Ibid., 2:37, 39-40.)

The only way in which we may gain exaltation is by receiving the blessings of the temple. All ordinances of the gospel are essential for a fulness of salvation, and the higher ordinances of the gospel are obtainable in the temple. In addition to the temple endowment, marriage for time and eternity opens the way for exaltation in the celestial kingdom. This blessing is dependent upon our faithfulness to the covenants received in the house of the Lord.

But faithfulness to gospel requirements does not begin in the temple. It is expected that those who enter that holy edifice are keeping the commandments as best they can. In addition to compliance with the principles of honesty, virtue, loyalty to authority, Word of Wisdom, and other principles of righteousness, the candidate for entrance to the temple is required to be a tithe payer. Thus we understand the importance of the fundamental requirement that for the highest blessings of salvation, one must be obedient to all principles of the gospel.

Why is it expected that a Latter-day Saint be a tithe payer to receive the temple ordinances? Can we believe that we should receive all that the gospel offers for salvation if we do not show that we are obedient to the law of tithing as well as to other commandments? President Anthon H. Lund said: "A man who professes to be a Latter-day Saint ought to show it in his works. If he does not pay his tithing, he shows there is something wrong with him. He cannot have the faith which he professes to have; for if he did he would not be delinquent in this matter. It is a matter between him and his God. There is no compulsion. But a man who has covenanted with the Lord to do His will cannot feel that he is honest with the Lord when he refuses to obey the calls He makes upon him." (*Conference Report*, April 1903, p. 24.)

Another requirement for male members of the Church who enter the temple is the holding of the Melchizedek Priesthood. Prior to a man's ordination for an office in this priesthood, he is interviewed to determine if he is living gospel laws of worthiness. This is so because this higher priesthood holds the keys to temple ordinances, the "mysteries of the kingdom," and the eventual knowledge of God, which is to become like him or to be exalted. (D&C 84:19; 132:24.) Again, one of the factors of worthiness is observance of the law of tithing. This requirement is further emphasized in the oath and covenant of the Melchizedek Priesthood of which each applicant for ordination is informed and which he covenants to live. The oath and covenant binds the ordained brother to two provisions: (1) to keep the commandments of the Lord and (2) to accept the duties of the office to which he is ordained in that priesthood. (D&C 84:33-40.) How can one not be a tithe payer and still keep the commandments of the Lord? How can one, under the oath and covenant, be a faithful holder of an ordained office in the priesthood and be negligent in paying his tithing?

The promise for faithfulness is this: "And he that receiveth my Father receiveth my Father's kingdom; therefore all that my Father hath shall be given unto him. And this is according to the oath and covenant which belongeth to the priesthood." (D&C 84:38-39.)

There are other covenants in the gospel of Jesus Christ that are binding upon the Saints. These covenants begin with the baptismal covenant and are renewed and kept in remembrance each time the sacrament is received. The Lord has said that if we do not abide by all the covenants received, then we are damned and are not permitted to enter into Christ's glory. (D&C 132:4-5.) The gospel, the new and everlasting covenant, "was instituted for the fulness of my glory; and he that receiveth a fulness thereof must and shall abide the law, or he shall be damned, saith the Lord God." (D&C 132:6.) The sacramental covenant includes the keeping of the commandments and a sincere willingness to "live by every word that proceedeth forth from the mouth of God." (D&C 20:77; 84:44.) In reminding the members of the Church of the need to keep the sacramental covenants, President Joseph Fielding Smith said: "If a man fully realized what it means when he partakes of the sacrament, that he covenants to take upon him the name of Jesus Christ and to always remember him and keep his commandments, and this vow is renewed week by week—do you think such a man will fail to pay his tithing? Do you think such a man will break the Sabbath day or disregard the Word of Wisdom? Do you think he will fail to be prayerful, and that he will not attend his quorum duties and other duties in the Church? It seems to me that such a thing as a violation of these sacred principles and duties is impossible when a man knows what it means to make such vows week by week unto the Lord and before the saints." (*Doctrines of Salvation*, 2:346.)

The last verse of the Latter-day Saint hymn "Praise to the Man" refers to the Prophet Joseph Smith's sacrifice of his life as a final testimony that God called him as the prophet of the dispensation of the fulness of times. The verse begins with these words: "Sacrifice brings forth the blessings of heaven." The greatest of all sacrifices is the giving of one's life. (Matthew 10:39; D&C 98:13.) Viewed from an eternal perspective, there is no sacrifice made in mortality that can equal the blessings the Lord has in store for those who are faithful to the end.

President Brigham Young declared: "With regard to Tithing, we give you the truth just as it is written in heaven, and just as you will find it by and by. What object have I in saying to the Latter-day Saints, do this, that or the other? It is for my own benefit, it is for your benefit; it is for my own wealth and happiness, and for your wealth and happiness that we pay Tithing and render obedience to any requirement of Heaven. We can not add anything to the Lord by doing these things. Tell about making sacrifices for the kingdom of heaven. There is no man who ever made a sacrifice on this earth for the kingdom of heaven, that I know anything about, except the Savior. He drank the bitter cup to the dregs, and tasted for every man and for every woman, and redeemed the earth and all things upon it. But he was God in the flesh, or he could not have endured it. 'But we suffer, we sacrifice, we give something, we have preached so long.' What for? 'Why, for the Lord.' I would not give the ashes of a rye straw for the man who feels that he is making sacrifices for God. We are doing this for our own happiness, welfare and exaltation, and for nobody else's. This is the fact, and what we do we do for the salvation of the inhabitants of the earth, not for the salvation of the heavens, the angels, or the Gods." (*Journal of Discourses*, 16:114.)

6

FAITH PRECEDES
THE PROMISE

"No man should attempt to excuse himself because he has this failing or that. If we have a failing, if we have a weakness, there is where we should concentrate, with a desire to overcome, until we master and conquer. If a man feels that it is hard for him to pay his tithing, then that is the thing he should do, until he learns to pay his tithing." (Joseph Fielding Smith, *Conference Report*, October 1941, p. 95.)

Lack of obedience to gospel principles is due essentially to a lack of faith in the Lord Jesus Christ. The knowledgeable Latter-day Saint knows that one may believe that God's promises are fulfilled, but belief does not always bring obedience to warrant receipt of those blessings. One may also have a knowledge of gospel principles, but as Elder John A. Widtsoe, an apostle of this dispensation, said:

"Knowledge tested and tried is the beginning of faith. For that reason 'it is impossible for a man to be saved in ignorance.' The extent of a person's faith depends in part on the amount of his knowledge. The more knowledge he gathers, the more extensive becomes his field of faith.

"The degree of faith possessed by any man depends not upon the extent of his knowledge, but upon the certainty of his knowledge, which leads to the proper use of his knowledge. Thus a man of great knowledge may have weak faith, while one of limited information may have strong faith. [Alma 32:34-41.]" (*Joseph Smith*, Bookcraft, 1957, p. 163.)

Moroni, the Book of Mormon prophet, wrote concerning the necessity of exercising faith in the promises of the Lord. He said that Jesus prepared the way, "that thereby others might be partakers of the heavenly gift, that they might hope for those things which they have not seen. Wherefore, ye may also have hope, and be partakers of the gift, if ye will but have faith." (Ether 12:8-9.)

To receive the blessings of heaven, we must have faith. As an example, Moroni cited the experience of the three Nephites who were granted their desire to live and teach salvation until the

38

Lord's second coming because of their faith, but "they obtained not the promise until after their faith." (Ether 12:17.)

Membership in The Church of Jesus Christ of Latter-day Saints requires faith in Jesus Christ and his atonement as a necessary condition preceding repentance and baptism. However, many members of the Church have never exercised strong faith in joining the Church as children or as converts. As a result, they have failed to obey some of the Lord's commandments. On the other hand, the member who begins with weak faith can develop into a person of strong faith through diligence and obedience. The apostle Paul said that faith "is the substance of things hoped for, the evidence of things not seen" (Hebrews 11:1), which means that faith is the positive assurance that we will receive from God those things which we righteously desire. An example of this kind of faith is the raising of Lazarus, who had died. When his sister Martha heard that Jesus was coming, she went out to meet him with this expression of perfect trust and faith: "Lord, if thou hadst been here, my brother had not died. But I know, that even now, whatsoever thou wilt ask of God, God will give it thee." (John 11:21-22.)

In order to develop true faith in God and the plan of salvation, the Prophet Joseph Smith said that three things were necessary: (1) the idea that God exists; (2) a correct understanding of his character, perfections, and attributes; and (3) a knowledge that the person seeking such faith is pursuing a course of life in accordance with the Lord's will. Otherwise, "the faith of every rational being must be imperfect and unproductive." (*Lectures on Faith,* Lecture 3, no. 5.) Though we might discuss many of God's attributes that contribute to our faith in him, these two from the Prophet seem to be essential:

". . . without the knowledge of all things, God would not be able to save any portion of his creatures; for it is by reason of the knowledge which he has of all things, from the beginning to the end, that enables him to give that understanding to his creatures by which they are made partakers of eternal life; and if it were not for the idea existing in the minds of men that God had all knowledge it would be impossible for them to exercise faith in him.

". . . for unless God had power over all things, and was able by his power to control all things, and thereby deliver his creatures who put their trust in him from the power of all beings that might seek their destruction, whether in heaven, on earth, or in hell, men could not be saved. But with the idea of the existence of this attribute planted in the mind, men feel as though they had nothing to fear who put their trust in God, believing that he has power to save all who come to him to the very uttermost." (*Lectures on Faith,* Lecture 4, nos. 11, 12.)

The Latter-day Saint who, by his faith, has proved that tithing is the way to receive blessings in this life may know that there are many reasons for paying tithing that add to his determination to continue to observe this law. These reasons may become incentives for others to follow so they too may grow in sufficient faith to become full tithe payers. Knowledge that the law of tithing is to be lived as a condition of the highest blessings in the gospel of Jesus Christ comes from keeping the commandments. It was President Brigham Young who said: "I know nothing about faith in the Lord, without works corresponding therewith; they must go together, for without works you cannot prove that faith exists. We might cry out, until the day of our death, that we love the Savior, but if we neglected to observe his sayings he would not believe us." (*Journal of Discourses,* 17:40.)

If we were to give priority to the reasons for being a tithe payer, certainly those given in the last chapter would be primary, because the ultimate in gospel salvation is to receive exaltation in the Father's kingdom. Other important reasons become incentives also to help us obey this law and understand how far-reaching the implications of obedience to the law of tithing are.

One reason is the need to sustain those who preside over the Church. The message of the prophets, seers, and revelators throughout the dispensations has been to follow the Lord's counsel in all things. Their concern is only for the welfare of the members of the Church. When we understand that our welfare is the paramount objective of the Church, local or general, there is sufficient reason for following the leaders' counsel.

Do we sustain our leaders if we do not follow their teachings? President Joseph F. Smith said: "And I cannot emphasize too strongly the importance of Latter-day Saints honoring and sustaining in truth and in deed the authority of the Holy Priesthood which is called to preside. The moment a spirit enters the heart of a member to refrain from sustaining the constituted authorities of

40 the Church, that moment he becomes possessed of a spirit which inclines to rebellion or dissension; and if he permits that spirit to take a firm root in his mind, it will eventually lead him into darkness and apostasy." (*Gospel Doctrine*, p. 224.)

Members of the Church must follow the counsel of the Lord's servants, whose voices, the Lord has revealed, are the same as his. Those who reject his servants' counsel are not blessed, for they pollute his holy words. (D&C 124:45-46.) Do we believe that this principle is a sufficient incentive to obey the law of tithing? What would our reaction be to the encouragement of our bishop to pay tithing if he called us into his office and counseled us to become full tithe payers? Would we believe that he is endeavoring to bestow blessings upon us by so doing? Is our faith in Jesus Christ sufficient enough for us to accept the teachings of his servants?

A fundamental principle of the gospel is that everyone is dependent upon the Lord. Everything we possess—food, raiment, money, gifts, talents—comes from the Lord. (Mosiah 4:19-21.) When viewed from the vantage point of our premortality and the purpose of life, it is clear that the opportunity to receive a body on an earth where we may work out our salvation has been provided for us by our Heavenly Father so that we might benefit eternally, if we are faithful. Those who obey the commandments are promised an everlasting inheritance upon this earth when it is celestialized. (D&C 38:17-20.) These truths suggest that through our obedience to the commandments, the Lord not only blesses us with salvation in the eternal worlds, but he also blesses us in this life with temporal blessings. Elder James E. Talmage wrote about the obligation we have to the Lord in the use of the earth and the things thereof:

"As the matter presents to my mind, it is as though there had been a contract made between myself and the Lord, and that in effect He had said to me—You have need of many things in this world—food, clothing, and shelter for your family and yourself, the common comforts of life, and the things that shall be conducive to refinement, to development, to righteous enjoyment. You desire material possessions to use for the assistance of others, and thereby gain greater blessings for yourself and yours. Now, you shall have the means of acquiring these things; but remember they are mine, and I require of you the payment of a rental upon that which I give into your hands. However, your life will not be one of uniform increase in substance and possessions; you will have your losses, as well as your gains; you will have your periods of trouble as well as your times of peace. Some years will be years of plenty unto you, and others will be years of scarcity. And now, instead of doing as mortal landlords do—require you to contract with them to pay in advance, whatever your fortunes or your prospects may be—you shall pay me not in advance, but when you have received; and you shall pay me in accordance with what you receive. If it so be that in one year your income is abundant, then you can afford to pay me a little more; and if it be so that the next year is one of distress and your income is not what it was, then you shall pay me less; and should it be that you are reduced to the utmost penury so that you have nothing coming in you will pay me nothing.

"Have you ever found a landlord of earth who was willing to make that kind of a contract with you? When I consider the liberality of it all, and the consideration that my Lord has had for me, I feel in my heart that I could scarcely raise my countenance to His heaven above if I tried to defraud Him out of that just rental.

"Consider further how therein and thereby He has provided that even the humblest may receive abundantly of the blessings of His house. The wealth of heaven is not reserved for the rich people of earth; even the poorest may be a stockholder in the great corporation of our God, organized for the carrying on of His purposes, in spreading the Gospel, in the building of Temples and other houses of worship to His name, and in doing good to all mankind." (*The Articles of Faith*, pp. 527-28.)

Elder Melvin J. Ballard gave the following wise observation about our partnership with the Lord: "The law of tithing is just and righteous. We need the blessing of the Lord today, of a material character. No man would think for a moment that he was not under obligation to pay rental to the owner for land that he tilled; and yet the owner cannot guarantee that the rain shall fall, that the snow shall come in the mountains, that the moisture so essential shall be provided, that the sun will shine, that the grain will germinate, that the harvest will come. Someone else must provide these essentials without which your farm is of little more value than an ash heap.

"Who provides these other important blessings? The Lord Almighty. Is he entitled to recognition and rental? Yes. The earth is the Lord's. It belongs to him, and we are but tenants. We owe him a rental, and he has enjoined upon us that a just rental is ten per cent of that which we obtain from the soil and from our labor." (*Conference Report,* October 1931, pp. 126-27.)

The Lord blesses the tithe payer as a partner with him because the "essence of partnership is a sharing of profits." However, there is also "a sharing of the burdens of the enterprise," and we cannot hope "to realize the profits from that venture without bearing his portion of the expense—the giving which is requisite." (Stephen L Richards, *Conference Report,* April 1929, p. 51.)

The material blessings that come from keeping the commandments, including tithing, may be realized in unusual ways, as suggested by Elder LeGrand Richards in citing an example from the life of President Heber J. Grant:

"I believe the Lord gives ideas to men who are liberal and men who have desires to serve God, and those who choose to serve the God of Israel rather than the God of mammon, and I remind you of President Grant's story. It impressed me when I was a boy. When he heard Bishop Woolley . . . in a fast meeting ask the Saints to be liberal in their contributions, he promised them that, if they would be liberal, the Lord would bless them four-fold.

"President Grant was then only a boy. He had fifty dollars in his pocket. He was working at the Zion's Savings Bank and intended to deposit it, but he handed it to the bishop, and the bishop wrote him a receipt for five dollars and gave him forty-five dollars change, but President Grant indicated that he wanted to pay it all. He wanted to put the Lord in his debt, because his mother needed two hundred dollars, and, if he paid fifty and he got four-fold, he would have his two hundred dollars. And Bishop Woolley said: 'Do you believe, Heber, that you will get your two hundred dollars sooner if you give this fifty dollars to the Lord?'

"He said, 'I do.' And the bishop wrote him a receipt for the other forty-five dollars, and on the way back to the bank he got an idea. Where did he get it from? He might never have received it had he not paid the fifty dollars. God Almighty sends ideas and he has regard for each one of his children individually. President Grant wired a man in the East, and in a few days he sold him enough bonds to make $218.50 profit, so when he paid the tithing on it the Lord had given him his two hundred dollars and almost enough to pay the tithing." (*Conference Report,* October 1948, pp. 45-46.)

The tithe payer cultivates thrift habits. "The payment of tithes of necessity compels an orderly arrangement of one's affairs. Accounting is indispensable. Budgeting is necessary. Saving follows. All of which are necessary to financial success. . . . I feel sure that he who pays his tithes not only has a better conception of economy, but he is indulging in a practice which will bring him into better thrift habits and enable him to go forward toward financial prosperity." (Stephen L Richards, *Conference Report,* April 1929, pp. 51-52.)

Elder Reed Smoot gave another reason for material blessings being received: "I believe that the man who pays his honest tithing to God will not only be blessed by God himself, but that the nine-tenths will reach farther than the other ten-tenths would if he had not obeyed that law; for the man who believes in the law of tithes and offerings, believes also in the other requirements made by God of him and he does not spend money in breaking the Sabbath day nor in going to places where his very soul is in danger of partaking of things that are not good for Latter-day Saints to receive." (*Conference Report,* October 1900, pp. 7-8.)

In time we must all stand before the judgment seat of God to be judged according to our works. If we have hardened our hearts "against the word, insomuch that it has not been found in us, then will our state be awful, for then we shall be condemned." (Alma 12:13.) In that day we shall acknowledge that all of his judgments are just, "that he is just in all his works, and that he is merciful unto the children of men, and that he has all power to save every man that believeth on his name and bringeth forth fruit meet for repentance." (Alma 12:15.) But what if death intervenes before faith brings repentance? Who knows the time of one's passing from this mortal sphere? The Lord gave this as a reason for obedience to his commandments: "And again I say, hearken unto my voice, lest death shall overtake you; in an hour when ye think not the summer shall be past, and the harvest ended, and your souls not saved." (D&C 45:2.)

In a general conference sermon President Spencer W. Kimball gave some examples of individuals who did not regard the keeping of the commandment to pay tithing as necessary. Concerning one such person who had amassed considerable property, he said:

" 'Did title come from God, Creator of the earth and the owner thereof? Did he get paid? Was it sold or leased or given to you? If gift, from whom? If sale, with what exchange or currency? If lease, do you make proper accounting?' "

"And then I asked, 'What was the price? With what treasures did you buy this farm?'

" 'Money!'

" 'Where did you get the money?'

" 'My toil, my sweat, my labor, and my strength.'

"And then I asked, 'Where did you get your strength to toil, your power to labor, your glands to sweat?'

"He spoke of food.

" 'Where did the food originate?'

" 'From sun and atmosphere and soil and water.'

" 'And who brought those elements here?'

"I quoted the psalmist: 'Thou, O God, didst send a plentiful rain, whereby thou didst confirm thine inheritance, when it was weary.' (Ps. 68:9.)

" 'If the land is not yours, then what accounting do you make to your landlord for his bounties? The scripture says: "Render unto Caesar that which is Caesar's and to God that which is God's." What percentage of your increase do you pay Caesar? And what percent to God? . . .'

"But my friend continued to mumble, 'Mine—mine,' as if to convince himself against the surer knowledge that he was at best a recreant renter.

"That was long years ago. I saw him lying in his death among luxurious furnishings in a palatial home. His had been a vast estate. And I folded his arms upon his breast, and drew down the little curtains over his eyes. I spoke at his funeral, and I followed the cortege from the good piece of earth he had claimed to his grave, a tiny, oblong area the length of a tall man, the width of a heavy one.

"Yesterday I saw that same estate, yellow in grain, green in lucerne, white in cotton, seemingly unmindful of him who had claimed it. Oh, puny man, see the busy ant moving the sands of the sea." (*Conference Report,* April 1968, pp. 73-74.)

Contrast that example with the faith demonstrated by President Joseph F. Smith's mother:

"I recollect most vividly a circumstance that occurred in the days of my childhood. My mother was a widow, with a large family to provide for. One spring when we opened our potato pits, she

had her boys get a load of the best potatoes and she took them to
the tithing office; potatoes were scarce that season. I was a little
boy at the time, and drove the team. When we drove up to the
steps of the tithing office, ready to unload the potatoes, one of the
clerks came out and said to my mother, 'Widow Smith, it's a
shame that you should have to pay tithing.' He said a number of
other things that I remember well, but they are not necessary for
me to repeat here. The first two letters of the name of that tithing
clerk were William Thompson, and he chided my mother for
paying her tithing, called her anything but wise or prudent; and
said there were others who were strong and able to work that were
supported from the tithing office. My mother turned upon him and
said: 'William, you ought to be ashamed of yourself. Would you
deny me a blessing? If I did not pay my tithing, I should expect the
Lord to withhold his blessings from me. I pay my tithing, not only
because it is a law of God, but because I expect a blessing by doing
it. By keeping this and other laws, I expect to prosper, and to be
able to provide for my family.'

"Though she was a widow, you may turn to the records of the
Church from the beginning unto the day of her death, and you will
find that she never received a farthing from the Church to help her
support herself and her family; but she paid in thousands of dollars
in wheat, potatoes, corn, vegetables, meat, etc. The tithes of her
sheep and cattle, the tenth pound of her butter, her tenth chick-
en, the tenth of her eggs, the tenth pig, the tenth calf, the tenth
colt—a tenth of everything she raised was paid. Here sits my
brother who can bear testimony to the truth of what I say, as can
others who knew her. She prospered because she obeyed the laws
of God. She had abundance to sustain her family. We never
lacked as much as many others did; for while we found nettle
greens most acceptable when we first came to the valley; and while
we enjoyed thistle roots, segoes and all that kind of thing, we were
no worse off than thousands of others, and not as poor as many, for
we were never without corn-meal and milk or butter, to my
knowledge. Then that widow had her name recorded in the book
of the law of the Lord. That widow was entitled to the privileges of
the house of God. No ordinance of the gospel could be denied her,
for she was obedient to the laws of God, and she would not fail in
her duty, though discouraged from observing a commandment of
God by one who was in an official position.

"This may be said to be personal. By some it may be considered egotistical. But I do not speak of it in that light. When William Thompson told my mother that she ought not to pay tithing, I thought he was one of the finest fellows in the world. I believed every word he said. I had to work and dig and toil myself. I had to help plow the ground, plant the potatoes, hoe the potatoes, dig the potatoes, and all like duties, and then to load up a big wagon-box full of the very best we had, leaving out the poor ones, and bringing the load to the tithing office, I thought in my childish way that it looked a little hard, specially when I saw certain of my playmates and early associates of childhood, playing round, riding horses and having good times, and who scarcely ever did a lick of work in their lives, and yet were being fed from the public crib. . . .

"Well, after I received a few years of experience, I was con-verted, I found that my mother was right and that William Thompson was wrong. He denied the faith, apostatized, left the country, and led away as many of his family as would go with him. I do not want you to deny me the privilege of being numbered with those who have the interests of Zion at heart, and who desire to contribute their proportion to the upbuilding of Zion, and for the maintenance of the work of the Lord in the earth. It is a blessing that I enjoy, and I do not propose that anybody shall deprive me of that pleasure." (*Gospel Doctrine*, Deseret Book Co., 1973, pp. 228-230.)

President Heber J. Grant, seventh president of the Church, gave this testimony regarding the law of tithing: "I am a firm believer that faith without works is dead, and I am a firm believer that the Lord meant what He said when He promised to open the windows of heaven and pour down a blessing on us if we would pay our tithing. . . .

"I believe, and believe it firmly, that among all the people of the Latter-day Saints who are in financial distress there are hardly any who have been honest tithe payers. Somehow or other God enlarges the capacity and ability of those who are liberal." (*Gospel Standards*, Improvement Era, 1969, p. 60.)

7

SPIRITUAL BLESSINGS

"The things of God should be surveyed by the light of the Spirit of God, not by the flickering candle of human wisdom. In our attitude toward divine revelations, the laws and ordinances of the Gospel, we should never take a shallow, material dollar-and-cent view, but always the higher, broader, deeper, spiritual view. . . . When we obey the Law of Tithing we do it not to please men, but to honor God, and we draw from Him, in return, a *spiritual dividend* far more precious and of much greater consequence than the dollars and cents or other means that we part with in rendering unto the Lord his own." (Orson F. Whitney, *Conference Report*, April 1931, pp. 64-65.)

A fundamental doctrine of the gospel is that of premortality, which means that every person lived as a spirit entity before being born into mortality. In that preexistence each person accepted the plan to come to earth and prove himself amid conditions that would prepare him for eternal life as a resurrected being. (Abraham 3:24-26.) The Lord revealed that only through the resurrection could a fulness of joy be received. (D&C 93:33-34.) The fulness of joy is the attainment of godhood or exaltation, which is the blessing that the spirit sons and daughters of God may receive by obedience to the laws of the gospel of Jesus Christ. (Moses 1:39; D&C 84:38; 88:106-107.)

Another basic doctrine is that the experiences and knowledge of this life continue with us into the next life. In other words, what we learn here becomes an integral part of the spirit being, which, in form, is like the individual person who lives on the earth. (D&C 130:18-19.) A person is the same in the spirit world as he was at death, for death does not change his character. (Alma 34: 32-34.) Consequently, the person who is disobedient to the commandments, or to even one of them, is to that degree under the influence of Satan. (Alma 34:35-36.) The vice or sin carried into the spirit world, whether it be indifference, selfishness, immorality, or disobedience to a commandment, continues as a part of that person's makeup. On the other hand, the virtues we develop through obedience to commandments also become a part of us, and in the spirit world we continue to strive to do the things of God.

During earth life, therefore, the physical body fashions, in a large measure, the character makeup of the spirit entity. The spirit may be willing, but the body may have ascendency if continued disobedience is accepted. (Matthew 26:41.) This principle explains why the prophets have counseled us to endure to the end and not to procrastinate our repentance. It also establishes a basis for the Lord's injunction that we become perfect in this life, even as he and the Father are perfect. (3 Nephi 12:48.) Concerning perfection President Joseph Fielding Smith said: ". . . I believe the Lord meant just what He said, that we should be perfect, as our Father in heaven is perfect. That will not come all at once, but line upon line and precept upon precept, example upon example, and even then not as long as we live in this mortal life, for we will have to go even beyond the grave before we reach that perfection and shall be like God.

"But here we lay the foundation. Here is where we are taught these simple truths of the Gospel of Jesus Christ, in this probationary state, to prepare us for that perfection. It is my duty, it is yours, to be better today than I was yesterday, and for you to be better today than you were yesterday, and better tomorrow than you were today. Why? Because we are on that road, if we are keeping the commandments of the Lord, we are on that road to perfection, and that can only come through obedience and the desire in our hearts to overcome the world." (*Conference Report,* October 1941, p. 95.)

We can become perfect in many principles of the gospel in this life. An excellent example is tithing. We know what is required of us in this commandment because it is a simple matter of arithmetic. It is an important contributor to the development of the spirit. Obedience to this law brings us closer to perfection, we enjoy a closer companionship of the Holy Spirit, and our spiritual powers grow.

As in every principle of the gospel, tithing is for man's benefit and not for the Lord's. President Wilford Woodruff stated: "Some of the people have looked upon the law of tithing as a kind of tax and burden laid upon them, but who is it for? Our tithing, our labor, and all that we do in the kingdom of God, who is it all for?

The tithing is not to exalt the Lord, or to feed or clothe him. I want the brethren to understand this one thing, that our tithing, our labor, our works are not for the exaltation of the Almighty, but they are for us. Not but what the Lord is pleased to see us obey his commandments, because by doing this it will place us in a position that will fulfill and accomplish the object of our creation, and bring about the end designed by our coming to take tabernacles here in the flesh. Again, when we do wrong, the Lord knows we shall inherit sorrow and misery if we continue in that wrong. Then I say, brethren, let us understand this as it is, and we shall do well. In paying our tithing, in obeying every law that is given to exalt us and to do us good, it is all for our individual benefit and the benefit of our children, and it is not of any particular benefit of the Lord, only as he is pleased in the faithfulness of his children and desires to see them walk in the path which leads to salvation and eternal life." (*Discourses of Wilford Woodruff*, p. 178-79.)

Wherein does the payment of tithing contribute to our coming nearer to our Heavenly Father? A relationship exists between all the principles and ordinances of the gospel. There is probably no virtue in the gospel that is not strengthened by the payment of tithing. For example, the tenth commandment received by Moses, "Thou shalt not covet," concerns a vice that is weakened and even destroyed if we faithfully live the principle of tithing. This commandment is, in turn, related to the other nine commandments. Elder Richard L. Evans explained:

"He who covets the mere material 'things' of life may have 'other gods before him,' and may 'bow down before them,' in thought and in spirit, if not in physical fact.

"He who covets may become coarse and careless in other things also, such as taking 'the name of the Lord God in vain.'

"He who covets may desecrate the Sabbath day to get gain.

"He who covets may fail to sustain his father and mother in their need.

"Some who have coveted have killed to get gain.

"Many who have coveted a 'neighbor's wife' have committed the grievous sin of adultery.

"He who covets is more likely to steal (or to swindle or embezzle or engage in sharp practices).

"He who covets may bear false witness to get gain.

"And so again: The tenth commandment is inseparably integrated with all the others, and coveting could lead to infraction of all the others—for there is a wholeness in life in which each part complements the others. And there is a wholeness and harmony in the word of God, and it all comes from the same source. And whenever we ignore any divine counsel or commandment, we can be sure that we weaken ourselves and increase our susceptibility to other sins." ("The Ten Commandments Today," M-Men *Gleaner Manual*, 1954-55, pp. 273-74.)

Selfishness is another vice that tithe paying can eliminate. The sacrifice of a portion of our means as tithing engenders generosity. The selfish person thinks of himself and not of the welfare of others. The tithe payer, on the other hand, has the welfare of others at heart as he contributes to the growth of the kingdom of God. No one can reach the ideal life of the Master and have only his own interests at heart. He must expand his vision and actions beyond the confines of his own pleasures. The Savior said: "Verily, I say unto you, Inasmuch as ye have done it unto one of the least of these my brethren, ye have done it unto me." (Matthew 25:40.) When a person is tempted to use his tithing contribution for other purposes, possibly for some pleasurable satisfaction, the overcoming of the temptation by paying his tithing develops in him greater spirituality and greater resistance against further such temptations.

Twofold blessings come to the tithe payer: temporal blessings of the things of this earth, and the more glorious blessing of being added upon as an exalted being who has an everlasting inheritance upon the celestialized earth. (Malachi 3:10-12; D&C 88:25-26.) Great is the promise to those who give thanks for all things. "And he who receiveth all things with thankfulness shall be made glorious; and the things of this earth shall be added unto him, even an hundred fold, yea, more." (D&C 78:19.)

One of the better ways in which we can express gratitude or thankfulness to God for all we have is by paying the tithing that he has requested. This demonstrates willingness to give of ourselves, our time, and our energy.

Payment of tithing increases our faith in God and his promises. Every principle of the gospel lived, every virtue developed brings greater spiritual power. Faith is the ingredient that develops the power to overcome all obstacles on the way to perfection. Since faith is a gift of God through the atonement of Christ, obedience to a law of the gospel brings greater faith to accomplish the purpose of life.

When the Prophet Joseph Smith told Martin Van Buren, president of the United States, that the difference between the Latter-day Saints and other Christian people was that the Saints had the Holy Ghost, he gave the key to the reason members of the Church partake of the sacrament each week. As we renew the covenants made at baptism in partaking of the bread and water, which represent the Savior's atonement, we are promised that we may have the Holy Spirit with us if we are worthy. What constitutes worthiness in this case? Must we be perfect, without sin? No. In another revelation the Savior said that if we strive to keep the commandments, we are considered to be keeping the commandments. (D&C 46:8-9.) But we must always remember that striving means concentrated effort. When we work diligently to obey the commandments, the Lord gives us the strength needed to accomplish the task. As we seriously endeavor to pay tithing, the Holy Spirit becomes more and more a helper in our reaching the required perfection. The person who has not experienced the blessings of the tithe payer may not have the same incentive to obedience as the person who knows the sweetness of what the Holy Spirit may do for him.

Possession of a gift or gifts of the Holy Ghost becomes one of the most prized possessions of the faithful Latter-day Saint. If, for example, an elder in the Church finds it necessary to bless his wife and children in a time of crisis, such as illness, is he really prepared to officiate in the ordinance of administration of the sick if he is not striving with all his heart to be worthy before the Lord? President J. Reuben Clark, Jr., expressed the importance for the priesthood of the Church to be prepared by worthiness: "Brethren, may the Lord bless me and bless you, give you and me abundantly of his spirit, that will enable us, first, to recognize what we are, the representatives of God on earth, endowed with certain of his powers. Never forget that. And next, help us so to live that we may enjoy those powers and exercise them, and then we shall rear our families as they should be reared. We will heal them when they are sick. We will be protected from harm and accident and disease. We will have more happiness than any of us can now imagine, all subject to the will of the Lord." (*Conference Report,* October 1955, p. 88.)

Many are the gifts of the Holy Ghost in addition to the gifts of faith to heal and to be healed. (D&C 46:19-20.) Among those gifts that are particularly beneficial for the person who seeks to be worthy of them are: diversities of operations, Word of Wisdom, word of knowledge, and discerning of spirits. (D&C 46:16-18, 23.) Appreciation of the purpose of each of these gifts and the Lord's beneficence should be expressed in a desire to live nearer and nearer to him. All of these gifts make the parent better prepared to rear his children in light and truth. (D&C 93:38-40.) Which Latter-day Saint would not prize the ability to discern the difference between false and true influences? In today's world where there are so many satanic ideas to deceive, the significance of the gift of diversities of operations, as well as the gift of wisdom in understanding better the problems and solutions that confront a family, should be apparent to all. With regard to the gift of wisdom, President Stephen L Richards said: "Wisdom is sometimes defined as sound judgment and a high degree of knowledge. I define wisdom as being the beneficient application of knowledge in decision. I think of wisdom not in the abstract but as functional. Life is largely made up of choices and determinations, and I can think of no wisdom that does not contemplate the good of man and society. Wisdom is true understanding." (*Conference Report*, April 1950, pp. 163-64.)

How many of us would appreciate the ability to instruct our children and others in wisdom? Such is the opportunity of those who possess the gift of the word of knowledge. The gift of discerning of spirits is different from the gift of diversities of operations, which refers to influences arising from knowledge. Discerning of spirits pertains to those influences which may control a person's thoughts and actions when under the power of evil spirits. Another gift of the Spirit that each individual must receive is the gift "to know that Jesus Christ is the Son of God." (D&C 46:13.)

How firm and stable is the testimony of a person who professes belief in a principle of the gospel but who does not practice it? Can we testify to the truth of the fulness of the gospel of Jesus Christ if we are not striving sincerely to live those truths? President Harold B. Lee said: "All principles and ordinances of the gospel are in a sense but invitations to learning the gospel by the practice of its teachings. No person knows the principle of tithing until he pays tithing." (*Stand Ye in Holy Places*, Deseret Book, 1974, p. 215.)

The fulness of blessings comes when we hearken to the counsel of those who preside over us. They admonish us to live the commandments, including tithing, in order to be full recipients of God's light and blessings. President Lee declared: "I have learned something of what the Spirit has taught, and I know now that the place of safety in this world is not in any given place; it doesn't make so much difference where we live; but the all-important thing is how we live, and I have found that security can come to Israel only when they keep the commandments, when they live so that they can enjoy the companionship, the direction, the comfort, and the guidance of the Holy Spirit of the Lord, when they are willing to listen to these men whom God has set here to preside as His mouthpieces, and when we obey the counsels of the Church." (*Conference Report,* April 1943, p. 129.)

If we do not now have the strong, abiding testimony described above, the Lord has provided the gift of believing the words of those who can testify of the truth. (D&C 46:14.) As we develop the gift to believe, it becomes easier for us to accept the counsel of the prophets and to thereby act upon their inspired teachings. When a father is striving to keep the commandments, his ability is increased to the point at which he can impart to his children the feeling that the Lord's truth is the only secure knowledge that leads to joy and happiness in life and forever.

From the companionship of the Holy Spirit comes spiritual understanding, one of the great spiritual dividends of the gospel. The spirit of revelation to know the simplest things as well as the greatest is the blessing of the faithful. One who has such a gift need not be led by every wind of doctrine in a world flooded with evil. He also has a clear conscience before man and God because he knows the purpose of life and is striving to fulfill that purpose. The obedient in this world receive peace because of the influence of the Spirit. This blessing is a spiritual dividend worth more than dollars and cents can ever buy. Accompanying peace of mind is the eternal reward of exaltation with the Father and the Son and with all who have also striven to become perfect.

President Stephen L Richards wrote: "Observance of tithing brings spiritual power, and after all that to me is the main thing. Religion is more than mere repose or relaxation. It is positive spiritual exercise. It makes for the growth of the soul, it cultivates all of the virtues. So one who is serious about religion will be

54

willing to give to it the things which are necessary and the things which are vital to himself." (*Conference Report*, April 1929, p. 52.)

Another testimony of the spiritual and temporal blessings that come to the tithe payer was given by Elder Reed Smoot: "I want to leave my testimony that God has given us the law of tithing, and He blesses the person that lives strictly in accordance with it. The blessings of the Lord are upon those who pay their tithing, no matter what the amount may be. I testify to you that people who live to this law have more comfort and peace in their homes, are more contented in their souls, have more faith that the Lord will answer their prayers, have more pleasure in fulfilling the requirements of the Church, and more confidence in the promises of God, than those who do not live this law. It is but natural that this should be so. I thank the Lord that my parents believed in the law of tithing. I thank the Lord that the first means which God ever placed into my hands, I had a mother who watched over me so carefully that she taught and guided me to pay my tithing on the same. I received this principle from my parents not only by precept, but by example as well, for they lived the law, because they had implicit faith in the God they worshipped." (*Conference Report*, October 1901, p. 5.)

8

FOR BUILDING THE KINGDOM OF GOD

"The law of tithing is a test by which the people as individuals shall be proved. Any man who fails to observe this principle shall be known as a man who is indifferent to the welfare of Zion, who neglects his duty as a member of the Church, and who does nothing toward the accomplishment of the temporal advancement of the kingdom of God. He contributes nothing, either, toward spreading the gospel to the nations of the earth, and he neglects to do that which would entitle him to receive the blessings and ordinances of the gospel." (Joseph F. Smith, *Gospel Doctrine*, p. 226.)

At baptism the Latter-day Saint covenants with the Lord to keep the commandments, to take upon himself the name of the Savior, and to always remember him; therefore, he should strive to always be on the Lord's side. (D&C 42:78; 20:77, 79.) President George Albert Smith, eighth president of the Church, related some counsel given to him by his grandfather, Elder George A. Smith: "There is a line of demarcation well defined between the Lord's territory and the devil's territory. If you will remain on the Lord's side of the line, the adversary cannot come there to tempt you. You are perfectly safe as long as you stay on the Lord's side of the line. But . . . if you cross to the devil's side of the line, you are in his territory, and you are in his power, and he will work on you to get you just as far from that line as he possibly can, knowing that he can only succeed in destroying you by keeping you away from the place where there is safety." (*Conference Report*, October 1945, p. 118.)

Why does Satan desire to keep us on his side of the line? His avowed intention is to fight the plan of salvation and destroy the work of the Lord in bringing his children to exaltation in the celestial kingdom. In a modern revelation, the Prophet Joseph Smith and Sidney Rigdon recorded that they saw that Satan "maketh war with the saints of God, and encompasseth them round about." (D&C 76:29.) It would be difficult to find a better description of the efforts of the devil in bringing the Saints into his bondage. Every principle of the gospel ignored is a victory for the evil one. His efforts are directed from every side at the members of the Church. False ideas regarding a fundamental principle of the gospel may prevent one from becoming a true disciple of the Lord. In his vision of Satan's efforts to keep people from the tree of life, Nephi saw the "temptations of the devil, which blindeth the eyes, and hardeneth the hearts of the children of men, and leadeth them away into broad roads, that they perish and are lost." (1 Nephi 12:17.)

False notions about how tithing is spent is one way in which Satan influences some members of the Church. Charges have long been made by enemies of the Church that "tithing is a system of extortion practiced upon the people for the enrichment of the priesthood." The First Presidency stated that tithing "operates upon the principle of free will and the consent of those who hold the faith to be divine." (*Improvement Era,* May 1907, pp. 481f.) In the April 1911 general conference they gave this evaluation of the false charges: "All the monstrous tales told of the wealth at the command of the heads of the Church are distorted emanations from disordered brains, or willful untruths manufactured in order to deceive the public."

There was a time when it was said that the Church was too materialistic. Christian churches have been prone to consider spiritual salvation as practically the only salvation the gospel demands. In a recent article entitled "Why Your Neighbor Joined the Mormon Church," a clergyman describes the way in which The Church of Jesus Christ of Latter-day Saints takes care of its members' temporal needs. He then observes that New Testament passages dealing with church finances show that "the basic use of the Lord's money was to meet the material needs of God's people (Acts 11:29; 1 Cor. 16:1-3)," and indicates that these matters had been passed over in the budgets of the Christian churches. (*Christianity Today,* October 11, 1974.)

A basic concept of the gospel of Jesus Christ is that all matters relating to our temporal existence also have a spiritual meaning. The Lord said he had never given a law that was temporal only. (D&C 29:34-35.) The payment of tithing is a spiritual act, because it indicates obedience to a spiritual commandment. Mormonism is a practical religion concerned with man every day, not just on Sunday. This was emphasized by Elder Albert E. Bowen:

"We have a very practical religion. It pertains to our lives now. And the reward of observance of the law is not altogether postponed to a future on the other side of the grave. Building up the kingdom involves some very practical things. It is not altogether concerned with the non-material lying out in the ethereal realm, . . . I do not think I can find the line that divides the spiritual from the temporal." (*Conference Report*, April 1951, p. 124.) In the gospel plan, the working out of our temporal salvation is a necessary part of our eternal salvation, because we are eternal beings living always in eternity.

Many times the revelations in the Doctrine and Covenants instruct the Latter-day Saints to participate in temporal matters, such as contributing funds to purchase property (D&C 90:28-29), paying off the mortgage on a farm (D&C 96:6-9), and building certain buildings (D&C 94:3, 10-12). Also, stewardships were assigned to some members for them to furnish, use, or manage. (D&C 104:19-46.)

Through the years the Church has owned properties, based on revelation, that have produced income. For example, the Lord commanded that the Nauvoo House be built as "a delightful habitation for man, and a resting-place for the weary traveler, that he may contemplate the glory of Zion, and the glory of this, the cornerstone thereof." (D&C 124:60.) In this same revelation a number of the brethren are called upon to "pay stock" in that house if they are "believer[s] in the Book of Mormon." (D&C 124:22-24, 119.) President Joseph F. Smith encouraged members to pay their tithing to help build up the area around the temple grounds in Salt Lake City. Concerning some of this property, he explained in general conference, "we have built upon it [Hotel Utah] and now it pays for itself, or meets its own obligations and helps the Church just a little. We have helped to build one of the most magnificent hotels that exists on the continent of America. . . . I am told that it is equal to any in the world, in its facilities for convenience and comfort for its guests, for sanitation, for its situation, and architectural beauty, and in many other ways. Well, some of our people have thought that we were extravagant. I would like you to turn to the book of Doctrine and Covenants and read the commandment of the Lord to the Prophet Joseph Smith in the city of Nauvoo. (See Doctrine and Covenants Section 124:22-24.) The people were requested to contribute of

58 their means to take stock in this building, and they and their children after them, from generation to generation, should have an inheritance in that building; for it was intended for the beauty of the city, for the glory of that stake of Zion, and to accommodate the stranger from afar who came to contemplate the doctrines of the Church and the work of the Lord." (*Conference Report,* October 1911, pp. 129-30.)

Another business enterprise sponsored by the Church for the benefit of the people was the sugar beet industry. President Heber J. Grant told a general conference that "many years ago President [Wilford] Woodruff announced that the Lord would like the great business of manufacturing sugar established in our midst." (*Gospel Standards,* p. 246.) Despite the negative counsel of some business leaders, President Woodruff declared, "And now the inspiration of the Lord to me is to build this factory. Every time I think of abandoning it there is darkness; and every time I think of building it, there is light. We will build the factory if it bursts the Church." Then President Grant added, "We did build it and it did not burst the Church. It and subsequent factories have made millions of dollars for our people." (Ibid., p. 248.)

In those pioneering days the Church sponsored enterprises, through inspiration from the Lord, that would benefit the people of the territory. President Joseph Fielding Smith wrote the following:

"It is, however, by divine revelation that the industries among the Latter-day Saints have been developed, and their leading men have set before them this example. It is by divine commandment that President Brigham Young and his brethren established the first commercial department store that was to be found in the borders of the United States. Did they do this with the thought in mind of becoming wealthy? Verily, no. The propelling thought back of it was to give employment, to furnish the members of the Church the necessities of life at reasonable rates and thus be benefited and protected from those who came to sell goods at excessive profits." (*Answers to Gospel Questions,* 3:78.)

In a general conference welfare agricultural meeting President Harold B. Lee referred to one classification of Church properties as welfare projects and said:

"We have another classification of properties which are revenue-producing. Some of these were originated back in the pioneer days when the Church got into things to help our people into farm-to-factory kind of crops like the sugar beet industry, ZCMI, banking, and such like. Many of those we have today originated way back for that purpose in the early rise of the Church when the Church had to originate much of its own commercial enterprise for the benefit of the people.

"Besides that, there are many revenue-producing properties which are held by the Church to protect our other properties like around temple block and the Church office building, where we very jealously guard the kind of neighbors we have, to make sure we don't have lounges and whatnot set up across the street from the temple. Not only here in Salt Lake but also elsewhere we jealously guard these properties that we want to hold as sacred properties. That's another classification that we have, and those, many of them, are revenue-producing properties on which we voluntarily pay taxes." (Address delivered October 3, 1970.)

President N. Eldon Tanner said that the Church does not own nor does it seek to control interest in any major national company. Furthermore, it does not buy securities in any corporation "that manufactures products such as cola drinks, publishing companies that print material that is not consistent with our standards, producers of alcoholic beverages, or tobacco companies." (*New Era*, July 1975, p. 50.) The Church owns some industries that help in the day-to-day work of the Church, including the Beehive Clothing Mills, *Deseret News*, and the Deseret Press. (Ibid.)

Among other things, the revenue-producing properties are used to pay the expenses of the General Authorities of the Church, who serve in a full-time capacity. When the Lord revealed the law of consecration, provision was made for those who labored in a full-time capacity for the Church to have their families supported out of the general funds of the United Order. (D&C 42:70-73.) Tithing, however, is not used to support the General Authorities. It is used to build up the kingdom of God upon the earth. President Joseph Fielding Smith said this about it: "Is it not better for the Authorities of the Church to receive compensation out of these industries and investments than to take it out of the tithing of the people? I am informed that the General Authorities of the Church are in no way paid out of the tithing of the Latter-day Saints. The tithes are used for the purposes for which they were originally intended. The compensation coming

60 from these investments helps to pay for the building of chapels, temples, and other edifices, thus lessening the burden that otherwise would be placed upon the people. (*Answers to Gospel Questions*, 3:78-79.)

In answering criticism concerning the General Authorities spending full-time in church service as do ministers in other churches, President Smith said: "Unfortunately there are those who seem to take delight in offering criticism and in finding fault without knowing the true conditions. Perhaps other churches would be better off, spiritually and temporally, if their ministers assisted the members in establishing industries and thus helped them financially to better their conditions. It can be said also that the officers of the Church of Jesus Christ of Latter-day Saints who labor without salaries coming out of the pockets of the members, are just as spiritually minded, have just as good judgment and wisdom in directing the temporal as well as the spiritual welfare of the people, as are any of the ministers who spend their entire time in what may be called spiritual counsel. For instance, the bishops of our wards and the presidents of our stakes and other officers give their time freely without any monetary compensation paid by members of the Church. It is equally true that the young men and women who are distributed over the face of the earth as missionaries of the Church pay their own way, or their parents do. We do not have a paid ministry, yet these brethren put in as much time in spiritual and Church duties, as do ministers of other denominations who devote their entire time, and in addition, they are under the necessity of earning their own living by their daily employment in industry. They do this because they have an abiding testimony of the divinity of the work the Church requires of them." (*Answers to Gospel Questions*, 3:79.)

The Lord instructed his seventy, who were to precede him into the villages where he would preach, to receive what assistance they needed from those who would offer it, "for the labourer is worthy of his hire." (Luke 10:1-10.) This truth was reiterated by the Lord in this dispensation, recognizing that those who work for the welfare of their fellow members should receive in accordance with their needs. This law applies to those who labor in temporal as well as in spiritual callings. (D&C 70:12-13.) Shortly after the Church was organized, three branches were told to support the Prophet Joseph Smith temporally in order that he might perform his calling as prophet. (D&C 24:3.) Remuneration for services was also given to certain groups during the Prophet's lifetime. (*History of the Church,* 1:220.) The number of persons who are in this category in the Church today are relatively few. The majority of the members function in the priesthood without monetary help. All members are expected to contribute of their time, talents, and material possessions for the advancement of the kingdom of God.

How is the tithing disbursed? The answer is found in a modern revelation: "Verily, thus saith the Lord, the time is now come, that it [tithing] shall be disposed of by a council, composed of the First Presidency of my Church, and of the bishop and his council, and by my high council; and by mine own voice unto them, saith the Lord. Even so. Amen." (D&C 120.) "The bishop and his council" are the Presiding Bishopric, and "my high council" is the Council of the Twelve Apostles. (D&C 107:15, 33.) In his calling as the prophet, seer, and revelator, the president of the Church is sustained in general conference as Trustee-in-Trust with the responsibility of controlling the funds and properties of the Church.

The careful manner in which the funds of the Church are disbursed was given by Bishop Joseph L. Wirthlin, Presiding Bishop of the Church:

"And so in compliance with this revelation, a council called 'The Council for the Disbursement of Tithing,' composed of the First Presidency, the Council of the Twelve, and the Presiding Bishopric has been organized, and under the direction of this council for the disbursement of tithing there has been organized a budget committee composed of two members of the Council of the Twelve and a member of the Presiding Bishopric. Each year the budget committee analyzes the financial needs of the various departments of the Church from the point of view of eliminating unnecessary expenditures. The budget, when compiled, is presented to the council for the disbursement of tithing, where again the First Presidency and the members of the council analyze the budget very carefully to assure themselves of no extravagant spending, and under the direction of this council for the disbursement of tithing there is another committee called 'The Expenditure Committee' of the Church who are authorized to approve expenditures as they are required by the departments of the Church. This committee meets once a week. It is composed of the First Presidency, three members of the Twelve, and the Presiding

Bishopric. And over the fifteen years that I have had the privilege of being a member of this committee, I have been inspired and thrilled by the careful appropriating of Church funds. Civil government could well afford to follow the example of the expenditure committee of the priesthood government of the Lord Jesus Christ." (*Conference Report,* April 1953, p. 99.)

For what purpose are the tithes used? The answer to this question was given by the Lord in the revelation on tithing: "For the building of mine house, and for the laying of the foundation of Zion and for the priesthood, and for the debts of the Presidency of my Church." (D&C 119:2.)

By revelation, the principal obligation resting upon the Latter-day Saints is to "bring forth and establish the cause of Zion." (D&C 6:6.) Under this commandment the Church has three major responsibilities: (1) to preach the gospel, (2) to perfect the lives of the members of the Church, and (3) to make it possible for members of the Church to save their dead. The vast operations of the Church today are concerned with these responsibilities, and the expenditure of large amounts of money is necessary to fulfill them.

Inasmuch as the major source of revenue for the Church is tithing, what may be done in this regard is limited by the funds available. The preaching of the gospel and the perfecting of the lives of the members of the Church requires the construction of many buildings; maintenance of these buildings; internal and external communications and administration of the Church; publication of printed materials for the use of the missionaries and teachers of priesthood and auxiliary classes, many of which must be translated into foreign languages; the sponsoring of an educational system; and so forth. "The greatest portion of Church expenditures goes toward meetinghouse construction and maintenance and to the education system, which includes seminaries and institutes, Church schools in underdeveloped countries, Brigham Young University, and Ricks College. . . . All of the funds of the Church are considered sacred and dedicated to furthering our Father's work on the earth, and they are managed prayerfully and with inspiration." (N. Eldon Tanner, *New Era,* July 1975, p. 50.)

When one examines the specifics of these uses, he discovers that though they consist of material or temporal things, their main contribution is spiritual, for, as indicated earlier, our activities in life have a spiritual meaning when they are directed toward the purposes of life. (D&C 29:34-35.) For example, ward and branch chapels, though made of wood, brick, and mortar, are used for instruction in spiritual truths and the receiving of spiritual strength. The same may be said of the Church educational system, where the young people of the Church receive spiritual training and guidance along with their academic studies.

Temple building and the genealogical resources of the Church promote the spiritual welfare of those who use these means for their own salvation and that of their dead. When it is understood that each member of the Church must, in order to receive the highest blessings of the gospel, be diligent in performing sacred ordinances in the temple for his progenitors and in obtaining genealogical data regarding them, the need to pay tithing is evident. (D&C 128:8-18.)

In reference to the building of a temple in Jackson County, Missouri, the Lord said: "Yea, let it be built speedily, by the tithing of my people.

"Behold, this is the tithing and the sacrifice which I, the Lord, require at their hands, that there may be a house built unto me for the salvation of Zion—

"For a place of thanksgiving for all saints, and for a place of instruction for all those who are called to the work of the ministry in all their several callings and offices;

"That they may be perfected in the understanding of their ministry, in theory, in principle, and in doctrine, in all things pertaining to the kingdom of God on the earth, the keys of which kingdom have been conferred upon you." (D&C 97:11-14.)

One may also understand how tithing used in the building of temples gives the spiritual blessings needed for exaltation when he reads the words of Elder John A. Widtsoe: "Temple work, for example, gives a wonderful opportunity for keeping alive our spiritual knowledge and strength. . . . The mighty perspective of eternity is unraveled before us in the holy temples; we see time from its infinite beginning to its endless end; and the dream of eternal life is unfolded before us. Then I see more clearly my place amidst the things of the universe, my place among the purposes of God; I am better able to place myself where I belong, and I am better able to value and to weigh, to separate and to organize the common, ordinary duties of my life, so that the little things shall not oppress me or take away my vision of the greater things that God has given us." (*Conference Report,* April 1922, pp. 97-98.)

To aid members in their genealogical research, the Genealogical Department promotes the gathering of vital data from the countries of the world. This collection includes microfilms of church and civil records, books, and other publications of genealogical value.

President Joseph F. Smith described the law of tithing as the law of revenue of the Church: "The purpose of the law of tithing is similar to that of the law of revenue which is enacted by every state, every country, and every municipality in the world, I suppose. There is no such thing as an organization of men for any purpose of importance, without provisions for carrying out its designs. The law of tithing is the law of revenue for the Church of Jesus Christ of Latter-day Saints. Without it, it would be impossible to carry on the purposes of the Lord." (*Gospel Doctrine,* p. 226.)

President George Q. Cannon gave the following answer to members of the Church who do not understand the reason for certain measures or counsel, such as, for what the tithes are used:

"A faithful Latter-day Saint may not be able to understand all the movements of the Church nor all the motives of the authorities of the Church in giving counsel or in taking action upon different questions; but will a man of this character censure them, assail them or condemn them? Certainly not. He will be likely to say: 'I do not understand the reasons for this action; I do not see clearly what the presiding authorities have in view in doing this; but I will wait and learn more. This I do know, that this is the work of God and that these men are His servants and that they will not be permitted by Him to lead the Church astray or to commit any wrong of so serious a character as to endanger its progress or perpetuity.' This would undoubtedly be the feeling of a man living close to the Lord, because the testimony of God's spirit would bring this to His mind and make him feel sure that God had not forgotten nor forsaken His Church." (*Gospel Truth,* 1:234.)

The Lord has promised that if the devout member of the Church will pray for understanding, he will receive it. (D&C 42:61; 32:4.) Into the heart of the faithful Saint comes a peace in the knowledge that the Lord is directing his kingdom upon the earth and that those who direct the activities of the Church are appointed by him. (D&C 124: 45-46.)

9

TITHING AND THE HOME

"I pray that you may have wisdom to set your own homes in order today, not delaying. Set them in order while there is yet time. Call your families about you, and if you have failed in the past to give them an understanding of the purposes of life and a knowledge of the Gospel of our Lord, do it now, for I say to you as a servant of the Lord, they need it now, and they will need it from now on." (George Albert Smith, *Conference Report,* April 1937, p. 36.)

As Latter-day Saints, we know that we are on this earth to be educated in the principles of truth so that we may become perfect. (3 Nephi 12:48.) Our education is not only for time, but also for eternity. Latter-day Saint parents esteem their children as a part of the working out of their own salvation and as a part of their eternal family. Happy are those parents whose children have followed their righteous counsel and are preparing themselves not only for this life, but also for the never-ending existence beyond the grave.

One of the great blessings of parents is children who abide by the commandments so well that they are eligible to receive the ordinances of the temple for their own exaltation in the celestial kingdom. All their posterity, until mortality ends, will add blessings forever upon them if they have sought to train their children in light and truth.

Because some Latter-day Saints have not followed the counsel of the Lord in rearing their children, they do not receive the blessings of the fulness of the gospel. Frederick G. Williams, a leading authority of the Church during the days of the Prophet Joseph Smith, was told the cause of an affliction he suffered: "You have not taught your children light and truth, according to the commandments; and that wicked one hath power, as yet, over you, and this is the cause of your affliction. And now a commandment I give unto you— if you will be delivered you shall set in order your own house, for there are many things that are not right in your house." (D&C 93:42-43.) In this same revelation the Lord said that Satan takes away light and truth from the children of men because of "the tradition of their fathers." (Verse 39.) As Latter-day Saint parents, what kinds of tradition are we establishing in our homes? One of disobedience that makes it possible for Satan to gain further inroads into our family and sets the stage for diminished faith?

In general conference in October 1950 President George Albert Smith said: "What are we going to do? . . . set our own homes in order, to see if there is carelessness or indifference in them, teach our families, and unite them and make them happy in keeping the commandments of our Heavenly Father, because only on the condition of righteousness can even this great Church continue and endure to do the work that it has to do." (*Conference Report,* October 1950, p. 181.)

A threefold goal of all Saints should be to unite the family, to make the members thereof happy, and to further the work of the kingdom of God. One of the major ways we can fulfill our obligation to the Lord is by paying tithing, and the foregoing goals are fulfilled when tithing is paid. Tithe paying contributes to the unity of the family because all are striving for the same goals, because happiness reigns in the knowledge that blessings of a temporal and spiritual nature will be theirs, and because the one-tenth contribution of the family's income gives satisfaction and a feeling of accomplishment in helping to build God's kingdom.

Why have Latter-day Saint parents been commanded to prepare their children for baptism "and to walk uprightly before the Lord"? (D&C 68:25-28.) The Lord knows that the young learn fast and are easily influenced and that childhood is a period of intensive accumulation of knowledge. Children are trusting and must rely on their parents for the knowledge upon which true values are based. Impressions and habits formed early shape the observance of commandments in the future. "Train up a child in the way he should go: and when he is old, he will not depart from it." (Proverbs 22:6.)

Despite the wonderful programs the Church offers, the major responsibility of training children is, and must continue to be, that of parents in the home. No parent can divorce himself from this obligation. The everyday program in the home makes its impact upon those who reside together as a family and results in character formation that cannot be equalled in a one-or-two-church-meetings-a-week procedure.

Parents must begin early to build a spiritual reservoir of power that will sustain and strengthen each individual member of the family. The way to do this is given in the scripture: "Draw near unto me and I will draw near unto you; seek me diligently and ye shall find me; ask, and ye shall receive; knock, and it shall be opened unto you." (D&C 88:63.) Is it likely that the child will seek if the parents are not also seeking? Are not the chances for success in life likely to be greatly decreased if guidance in obedience to commandments is not taught early? Upon the heads of Latter-day Saint parents rests the responsibility to teach their children; if they do not, the sin will be upon their heads.

Does the admonition to find rest to one's soul early in life apply to everyone, young and old? Yes, the Lord's hand is stretched out to everyone, but if the opportunity comes early in life, there is greater opportunity for a person to change his habits and practices. We have heard persons later in life say, "If I had only known of the fulness of the gospel years ago! What a difference it would have made in my life!" How sad it is when Latter-day Saint parents hear this remark: "If my parents had only taught me these truths, what a difference it would have made in my life!"

Should a child pay tithing? Yes, "every man, woman and child, who earns and receives a return for labor...." (Joseph F. Smith, *Gospel Doctrine*, p. 228.) The amount of tithing is not important as long as it is a full tithe. The penny is as much a tithe as the hundreds of dollars. No one who receives an income is exempt—not the President of the Church, the apostle, the widow, or the child.

The counsel of Church leaders is to pay tithing when the income is received. Notice the wisdom of this counsel to parents and children: "I have found it to be a very difficult problem in mathematics to pay one-tenth out of one-twelfth. I commend that thought to those who are receiving monthly stipends and who indulge the practice of paying their tithing at the close of the year. I am sure you will find it very difficult indeed to get the tenth out of the twelfth if your tithing remains for payment until the last month. I can heartily recommend to you the payment of your tithes as your funds come into your hands, not only because it will be easier, but because greater blessings will inure to you." (Stephen L Richards, *Conference Report*, April 1929, p. 53.)

A habit of punctuality in paying one's tithing insures the payment. President Heber J. Grant said the Lord is different from

68 those in whose debt we are: "The Lord, you know, does not send collectors around once a month to collect bills. He does not send us our account once a month. We are trusted by the Lord. We are agents. We have our free will. And when the battle of life is over, we have had the ability and the power and the capactiy to have done those things which the Lord required us to do and we cannot blame anybody else." (*Gospel Standards*, p. 63.)

By teaching the law of tithing, parents can also teach the principle of honesty. Honesty should begin by paying to the Lord the debt each person incurs for the privilege of earth life and its many opportunities. The experience of many is that if one is honest with the Lord he will also be honest with his fellowmen. The testimony of Dr. Ernest L. Wilkinson, former president of Brigham Young University, illustrates the value of being honest and also points out the blessings that come from tithe paying:

"At the conclusion of my third year of law at the George Washington University, I had been blessed with the receipt of a scholarship at Harvard University for further advanced study in the law. I accordingly made arrangements to go to Harvard for an additional year of legal training. Preparatory to leaving Washington, I figured up my accounts and found that I was short some $230 in that year in the payment of tithing. Not wanting to leave that branch without making a full accounting to my branch president, I went to a strange bank in Washington, D.C., to see if I couldn't borrow $230. I approached the lending officer with a great deal of fear and apprehension. He did not know me, and I had established no credit at the bank. Indeed, I had no credit to establish. I thought the best thing to do under the circumstances was to tell him the reason for my wanting the loan. As I concluded telling him the reason, the banker looked at me and said, 'Young man, if you have enough character in you to consider that tithing is an obligation for which you need to borrow money, this bank will be happy to make the loan. We have no doubt you will repay it.'" ("The Principle and Practice of Paying Tithing," *Brigham Young University Bulletin*, vol. 54, no. 25, pp. 20-22.)

Sometimes parents find it difficult to maintain their families financially, and many go into debt. Every measure should be taken to avoid debt, though there may be times when credit must be sought to purchase essential items. Elder Marriner W. Merrill told this experience:

"I was conversing with a brother some three or four years ago. I think at the conference in this city, and he was telling me his condition. He was very much depressed financially. He had been under the necessity (he thought) to mortgage his home, and he was very much embarrassed. He felt very bad over it, so much so that he could hardly enjoy the spirit of the conference. He was a very intimate friend of mine, and he asked me what to do. I told him that I believed that I could tell him what to do to extricate himself. He said he would be very glad to know what to do that he might be free again. I said, 'Have you paid your tithing of late years?' 'Well,' he said, 'no, not so strictly as I ought to have done.' I told him I thought that was one cause of his financial trouble. I said to him, 'You go home now, and pay your tithing strictly as you receive it; don't you sign any more notes to anybody; don't give mortgages on any more of your property; curtail your expenses at home, retrench a little, for I believe there is room for retrenchment; pay your tithing; trust in the Lord, and ways will be opened up whereby you may extricate yourself.' I met him at this conference, and he said that he was getting along fine. He has nearly all of his debts paid, and he has lifted the mortgage from his home. I said, 'Then you have paid your tithing, have you?' He said, 'Yes, paid my tithing strictly and honestly.' " (Preston Nibley, ed., *Inspirational Talks for Youth*, pp. 288-89.)

Elder Robert L. Simpson, Assistant to the Council of the Twelve, related this experience: "I want to share with you the testimony of a wonderful brother who had been impressed by one of the Church leaders as he explained the law of tithing. Meeting him on the street about three months later, he took some money from his pocket and said: 'Do you see this? It is all mine. It does not belong to the butcher, the baker, or the loan agency. For the first time in my life I am free of debt. I can walk down either side of the street with my head held high. I no longer have to cross from side to side, avoiding the shopkeepers holding my delinquent accounts.' Then he went on to tell how all this came about because he took time to sit down with his family, and they decided how they were going to meet their obligation to the Lord." (*Conference Report*, April 1966, p. 53.)

Elder LeGrand Richards of the Council of the Twelve testified in the following manner concerning the Lord's promises being fulfilled:

"I have always said that when I was the Presiding Bishop, we did not place the paying of tithing in the youth program to obtain an individual award to get more money. We wanted every boy and girl in Israel to have their names recorded in the Lord's book of remembrance and to be numbered among his jewels.

"Speaking of doing all things whatsoever the Lord hath commanded, you will remember that the Lord said: 'I, the Lord, am bound when ye do what I say; but when ye do not what I say, ye have no promise.' (D&C 82:10.) So all we need to do is to know what the Lord says and then do it, and then we have the Lord's promise that he will make good.

"I could tell you many stories about tithing to let you know that the Lord doesn't fail. I have the faith that a man can keep out of debt longer, get out of debt easier, live more comfortably on the ninety cents on the dollar, with the blessing of the Lord, than on the dollar when he 'paddles his own canoe,' if you will let me put it into those words, because I have watched it, and I know that it works in the lives of people.

"Sister Richards and I toured the Scandinavian missions . . . and some of their leading men who joined the Church said that the one thing that held them back was the payment of tithing. 'Now,' they said, 'we have more money to spend than we have ever had in our lives. Now we can go to the temple and do other things that we never thought we could do before.' " (*Conference Report*, April 1961, p. 44.)

Blessings are received in the home by all who are obedient. The widow and the fatherless have great need for help. President Joseph F. Smith testified that the Lord is mindful of those in need who are determined to be obedient:

"I preach that which I believe and that which I do know to be true, and I do know that if men will obey the laws of God, God will honor and bless them. I have proven it all my life through. I saw it manifested in circumstances which occurred in my childhood, and I know that God has blessed the widow and the fatherless when they have been obedient to his laws and have kept his commandments.

"I can tell you the history of a widow woman, with a large family, who was more particular, if possible, to pay the Lord what belonged to him than she was to pay to her neighbors to whom she might be indebted, and she never was indebted to her neighbors, thank God, for anything that she did not pay to the last cent, because the Lord blessed her with plenty, and in her latter years she did not have to borrow of her neighbors, nor did she have to call upon the Church for support, either, but she paid thousands of dollars in products and money into the storehouse of the Lord, although she was a widow with a large family to support. I know this. I can testify of this, and that the Lord Almighty blessed her, not only in the products of her fields, but in her flocks and herds. They were not devoured. They were not destroyed. They did not lie down and die. They increased. They did not stray away; and thieves did not steal them. One reason for that was, she had a little boy that watched them very carefully under her direction, and prompting. Her eye was upon everything, she had supervision over everything, she directed those whom she employed, and her children; and I am a witness—and here sits another witness (Patriarch John Smith)—that God, the eternal Father, blessed her and prospered her while she lived, and she was not only enabled to maintain herself and children that were left to her in poverty, in a day of trial, and when she was driven out into the wilderness, but she was able to feed scores of the poor, and to pay her tithes besides. Verily the Lord prospered her, and she was blessed." (*Gospel Doctrine*, pp. 230-31.)

Preparations are made in the home to send sons or daughters into the mission field or to school, and sometimes the temptation is present to use tithing funds to support these efforts. The following lesson taught by President George Albert Smith sets forth the true concept of tithing. Following a stake conference he was accompanied home by a friend, and this conversation ensued:

" 'You know, I have heard many things in this conference, but there is only one thing that I do not understand the way you do.'

"I said: 'What is it?'

" 'Well,' he said, 'it is about paying tithing.'

"He thought I would ask him how he paid his tithing, but I did not. I thought if he wanted to tell me, he would. He said, 'Would you like me to tell you how I pay my tithing?'

"I said, 'If you want to, you may.'

" 'Well,' he said, 'if I make ten thousand dollars in a year, I put a thousand dollars in the bank for tithing. I know why it's there. Then when the bishop comes and wants me to make a contribution for the chapel or give him a check for a missionary who is going away, if I think he needs the money, I give him a check. If a family in the ward is in distress and needs coal or food or clothing or anything else, I write out a check. If I find a boy or a girl who is having difficulty getting through school in the East, I send a check. Little by little I exhaust the thousand dollars, and every dollar of it has gone where I know it has done good. Now, what do you think of that?'

" 'Well,' I said, 'do you want me to tell you what I think of it?'

"He said, 'Yes.'

"I said, 'I think you are a very generous man with someone else's property.' And he nearly tipped the car over.

"He said, 'What do you mean?'

"I said, 'You have an idea that you have paid your tithing?'

" 'Yes,' he said.

"I said, 'You have not paid any tithing. You have told me what you have done with the Lord's money but you have not told me that you have given anyone a penny of your own. He is the best partner you have in the world. He gives you everything you have, even the air you breathe. He has said you should take one-tenth of what comes to you and give it to the Church as directed by the Lord. You haven't done that; you have taken your best partner's money, and given it away.'

"Well, I will tell you there was quiet in the car for some time. We rode on to Salt Lake City and talked about other things.

"About a month after that I met him on the street. He came up, put his arm in mine, and said: 'Brother Smith, I am paying my tithing the same way you do.' I was very happy to hear that.

"Not long before he died, he came into my office to tell me what he was doing with his own money." (George Albert Smith, *Sharing the Gospel with Others,* Deseret Book Co., pp. 45-47.)

In summary, it can be said that the Lord has placed the obligation upon Latter-day Saints to rear their children in light and truth and to set before them proper examples. The effects of teaching correct principles to children are longlasting. Happy are the parents who diligently give every advantage to their children to begin life's journey on the way to perfection and who continue to encourage and help them become saints indeed. The earlier the process begins in the payment of tithing, the easier it becomes to inure children to other basic principles of the gospel. President Joseph F. Smith said: "Another requirement that I wish to mention is that the parents in Zion will be held responsible for the acts of their children, not only until they become eight years old but, perhaps, throughout all the lives of their children, provided they have neglected their duty to their children while they were under their care and guidance, and the parents were responsible for them." (*Conference Report*, April 1910, p. 6.)

10
TITHING
AND ZION

"And I say unto you, if my people observe not this law [tithing], to keep it holy, and by this law sanctify the land of Zion unto me, that my statutes and my judgments may be kept, thereon, that it may be most holy, behold, verily I say unto you, it shall not be a land of Zion unto you." (D&C 119:6.)

When the Lord gave the law of tithing in this dispensation, it was designed to bring the Saints closer to living the greater law of consecration. When the Lord gives a law and his people fail to live it, he desires to bring his people up to the standard of that law. So it is with tithing. If one thinks he has the ability to live a celestial law but he fails to observe a lesser law, he should reexamine his thinking and determine where he stands before the Lord.

The significance of the concept of Zion mentioned at the beginning of this chapter is well emphasized in modern revelation. Before the Church was organized in 1830, the Lord told Joseph Smith and Oliver Cowdery, "Now, as you have asked, behold, I say unto you, keep my commandments, and seek to bring forth and establish the cause of Zion; Seek not for riches but for wisdom, and behold, the mysteries of God shall be unfolded unto you, and then shall you be made rich. Behold, he that hath eternal life is rich." (D&C 6:6-7.)

Nephi considered the pursuit of wealth as contrary to the establishment of Zion: "But the laborer in Zion shall labor for Zion; for if they labor for money they shall perish." (2 Nephi 26:31.) President Anthon H. Lund elaborated on Nephi's statement: "He [Nephi] says that the people should work for Zion. That should be the object of their coming together, the one aim and purpose of their lives—to work for Zion, and not to make anything else the object of their lives. If they make money their object, He says they shall perish. How often have we seen this fulfilled! Those who have forgotten why the Lord called them from their homes and gathered them here, and who have made money their sole object, have perished spiritually; they have lost the faith which was once so strong in their breasts that they were able to leave everything that was dear unto them and gather here. . . . We want to be laborers in Zion, and work for the cause of Zion, and not for other objects—that is, not to make them the only objects of our lives." (*Conference Report,* October 1897, p. 3.)

The Prophet Joseph Smith said that the prophets of old "looked forward with joyful anticipation to the day in which we live; . . . we are the favored people that God has made choice of to bring about the Latter-day glory; it is left for us to see, participate in and help to roll forward the Latter-day glory. . . . the Spirit of God will be showered down from above, and it will dwell in our midst. The blessings of the Most High will rest upon our tabernacles, and our name will be handed down to future ages; our children will rise up and call us blessed; and generations yet unborn will dwell with peculiar delight upon the scenes that we have passed through, the privations that we have endured; the untiring zeal that we have manifested; the all but insurmountable difficulties that we have overcome in laying the foundation of a work that brought about the glory and blessing which they will realize; a work that God and angels have contemplated with delight for generations past; that fired the souls of the ancient patriarchs and prophets; a work that is destined to bring about the destruction of the powers of darkness, the renovation of earth, the glory of God, and the salvation of the human family." (*History of the Church,* 4:609-10.)

The complete fulfillment of the prophecies concerning the Lord's work will come when an appointed angel proclaims the downfall of evil: "It is finished; it is finished! The Lamb of God hath overcome and trodden the wine-press alone, even the wine-press of the fierceness of the wrath of Almighty God" (D&C 88:106), and all men have been resurrected and judged at the end of the earth (D&C 88:97-104).

Preparations for the coming of the Lord in power and glory are underway now as The Church of Jesus Christ of Latter-day Saints continues its mission in teaching all people, perfecting the lives of its members, and redeeming the dead. The purpose for the restoration of the Church is to prepare the people for the millennial reign of the Savior. We have the opportunity to be numbered among those who are prepared.

Whatever one does to build up the kingdom of God on earth and to work for the establishment of Zion brings him closer to the

76 realization of the purpose for which he was born. The people of Zion will assist the Lord in the great events of the last days. But how does one become numbered among those of Zion? The Lord said that "the pure in heart" are Zion. (D&C 97:21.) We must consecrate our time, talents, and whatever means are necessary to the Lord. If our feelings are centered in the principles of righteousness, we are pure in heart. Our standard of measuring righteous action should not be popular approval but divine approval. If we hunger and thirst after righteousness, the Holy Ghost implants righteousness in our souls. When we keep the commandments of the Lord, we retain a remission of our sins. (Mosiah 4:11-30.) In brief, we may say that the people of Zion are those who have accepted the atonement of Jesus Christ and abide in the truth. The difference between Zion and the world was expressed by President Stephen L Richards: "There is no fence around Zion or the world, but to one of discernment, they are separated more completely than if each were surrounded with high unscalable walls. Their underlying concepts, philosophies, and purposes are at complete variance one with the other. The philosophy of the world is self-sufficient, egotistical, materialistic, and skeptical. The philosophy of Zion is humility, not servility, but a willing recognition of the sovereignty of God and dependence on his providence." (*Conference Report,* October 1951, p. 110.)

There are some converts to the Church who feel that the society into which they have come is not equal with their expectations of the people of Zion. One should keep in mind that it is the contributions of the many that bring about such a condition. The blessings come to those who feel that they individually must make a contribution to the building of a Zion environment and thus save themselves. To make Zion within oneself, said President Brigham Young, should be the goal of all members of the Church, saying to themselves, " 'I will carry myself full of the Spirit of Zion wherever I go; and this is the way in which I will control evil spirits; for I mean that my spirit shall have control over evil,' and do you not see that such a course will make Zion?" (*Journal of Discourses,* 5:4.) The blessing of being sanctified does not come immediately; it takes time to overcome one's failings.

Some of the Nephites put forth the effort and achieved this state of existence: "Nevertheless they did fast and pray oft, and did wax stronger and stronger in their humility, and firmer and firmer in the faith of Christ, unto the filling their souls with joy and consolation, yea, even to the purifying and the sanctification of their hearts, which sanctification cometh because of their yielding their hearts unto God." (Helaman 3:35.)

To be "born again" through baptism is the process by which sanctification comes. This birth makes church members "new creatures; and unless they do this, they can in nowise inherit the kingdom of God." (Mosiah 27:26.) As one reads the experiences of other Nephites in effecting a mighty change in their hearts and becoming spiritually reborn, a greater understanding of the totality of this rebirth is realized. In effect, sanctification comes by strict obedience to the will of God, learning of his teachings, being susceptible to the promptings of the Holy Ghost, following the teachings of the prophets, and enduring to the end.

The people of Zion are found where the saints of God are gathered throughout the world, "armed with righteousness and with the power of God in great glory." (1 Nephi 14:14.) Many Saints, knowing of the prophecies concerning the eventual building of the center place of Zion, or the New Jerusalem, look forward to the day when this great city will be built. (3 Nephi 21:10-23; Ether 13:2-11; D&C 45:66-67.) It will be one of two capitals of the world when, during the millennium, the Savior will rule as King of kings and Lord of lords. (Micah 4:1-2; Revelation 17:14; D&C 45:57-59.) President Joseph F. Smith stressed the qualities of the people who would live there:

". . . and no man, so far as I know, can foretell the day or the hour, the month or the year when the people of God shall be ready to redeem Zion and build up the center stake. . . . It will be in the due time of the Lord, when the people of God are *prepared* to go back, and not before. Whether it be in this generation or in the next generation, it matters not; it will only be when the people have prepared themselves to do it by their faithfulness and obedience to the commands of God. I prophesy to you, in the name of the Lord, that when the Latter-day Saints have prepared themselves through righteousness to redeem Zion, they will accomplish that work and God will go with them. No power will then be able to prevent them from accomplishing that work; for the Lord has said it shall be done, and it will be done in the due time of the Lord, when the people are prepared for it.

"But when shall I be prepared to go there? Not while I have in my heart the love of this world more than the love of God. Not while I am possessed of that selfishness and greed that would induce me to cling to the world or my possessions in it, at the sacrifice of principle or truth. But when I am ready to say, 'Father, all that I have, myself included, is Thine; my time, my substance, everything that I possess is on the altar, to be used freely, agreeable to Thy holy will, and not my will, but Thine, be done,' then perhaps I will be prepared to go and help to redeem Zion." (*Millennial Star*, 56:385-86.)

The law of consecration (D&C 42:30-42), also known as the United Order, will be the celestial law operating in Zion. But what of those who do not obey the lesser law of tithing? President Joseph Fielding Smith said: "If we are stingy with the Lord, he may be stingy with us, or in other words, withhold his blessings. Then again, we have those among us who are hoping for the coming of the law of consecration thinking that in that day they are going to profit by the equalizing of the wealth of other members of the Church. It is definitely true, however, that all those who will not obey the law of tithing, will not be entitled to enter into the covenants of consecration, but when the day comes for the establishing of Zion and the redemption of the earth, such people will find themselves removed." (*Church History and Modern Revelation*, 2:92.)

Students of the Book of Mormon know the promises made concerning the land of America. The prophet Lehi was told that he and his colony would be led to a land that would be "choice above all other lands." (1 Nephi 2:20.) An angel gave to Lehi's son Nephi this same information concerning the land to which the Lehites would be divinely directed. The angel also told Nephi that it would be the land of his father's inheritance and that their seed would continue to live on that land. (1 Nephi 13:30; 2 Nephi 1:5.) The gentiles who would come to the land of America would also be blessed if they were righteous, and they would be free from bondage and captivity. (2 Nephi 10:10-14.) When Jacob blessed his son Joseph, he foresaw that the land we know as America would be a precious land, as did Moses when he blessed the tribe of Joseph. America was to be blessed richly with the products of the land and the mountains because it was the land of Zion. (Genesis 49:22-26; Deuteronomy 33:13-17; D&C 101:16-20.) Today, Zion exists not only in America but also wherever the saints of God are "armed with righteousness and with the power of God in great glory" because they keep the commandments of the Lord. (1 Nephi 14:14.)

The scriptures give several characteristics of Zion. The Lord has said that it will be "a land of peace, a city of refuge, a place of safety for the saints of the Most High God." (D&C 45:66.) What reigns in the households of Zion? In those homes the parents obey the Lord and seek to rear their children in light and truth. They are honest with the Lord in the payment of their tithes, and they give their children the advantages of early training in obedience to the commandments. The Lord called Enoch's people Zion because they were of "one heart and one mind." (Moses 7:18.)

When the modern city or land of Zion is established as the center place, there will be no poor there. In the meantime, however, Zion homes will be places where the Lord's temporal and spiritual blessings abide, because the members live celestial laws. The Lord's revelation is definite regarding the necessity of his people being tithe payers in order that the land might be sanctified as Zion: "And I say unto you, if my people observe not this law, to keep it holy, and by this law sanctify the land of Zion unto me, that my statutes and my judgments may be kept thereon, that it may be most holy, behold, verily I say unto you, it shall not be a land of Zion unto you. And this shall be an ensample unto all the stakes of Zion. Even so. Amen." (D&C 119:6-7.)

Only through living the principles of the celestial kingdom can Zion be enjoyed by those who have accepted Jesus Christ as their Savior. Unity is brought into the Church by members who follow the counsel of the living prophet to live the celestial laws. As one obeys the law of tithing and other commandments, he contributes to the well-being of the Church as well as to his own eternal salvation.

Elder James E. Talmage taught that "there is a relationship between the elements and forces of nature, and the actions of men." (*Conference Report*, October 1929, p. 68.) The promises made to the Jaredites and the Nephites on this continent were literally fulfilled when they kept the commandments of the Lord. They prospered both temporally and spiritually. When they disobeyed the commandments, however, and lived in wickedness, they suffered the loss of temporal blessings, and dire calamities overcame them because of their spiritual decline. These same predictions have been made concerning modern Zion. (D&C 97:25-26.)

To those who believe in the Lord's promises and to those who do not, President Joseph F. Smith said the following:

"No doubt, a good deal more could be read from the scriptures in relation to this principle of tithing, which God has revealed to us in this dispensation, and which he requires at our hands, that we may sanctify, by obedience to his law, this land that it may become indeed a land of Zion unto us; and the promise is, that if we will obey the laws of God, if we will put our trust in him, if we will draw near unto him he will draw near unto us, and he will reward us with his favor and his blessing. He will rebuke the devourer, and he will cause that the earth shall be fruitful, that it shall yield in its strength to the husbandman, the tiller of the soil, and to the herder of flocks. He will increase his kine, and will prosper him upon the right hand and upon the left, and he shall have an abundance, because he puts his trust in God; he draws near unto him, and he is willing to prove him, to see whether he will not open the windows of heaven and pour out blessings upon him that he shall not have room to contain them. Let every man who has received the gospel of Jesus Christ receive this saying, and hearken to these words, for all they are worth. Some men may esteem them lightly, and those who do, will, without doubt, fail to draw near, they will neglect to prove the Lord, they will not fulfil the commandments that he has given, and they will never know that God tells the truth, and that he is able to fulfil his word and promise unto his people when they are willing to obey and keep his law. While they who appreciate these promises, who obey these laws that were given anciently, and have been renewed again in the dispensation of the fulness of times, for the blessing of the people, for the building up of Zion, for the feeding of the widow and the orphan, or the spreading of the gospel of Christ to the nations of the earth, and for the gathering of the people from the four quarters of the earth, those who hearken to these words, prize them as the truth, and apply them in their practice throughout their lives, will come to know that God is a rewarder of those who diligently serve him, and that he is able to fulfil his promises unto them." (*Gospel Doctrine*, pp. 226-27.)

11

OFFERINGS UNTO THE LORD

"Now I think it is perfectly clear that the Lord expects far more of us than we sometimes render in response. We are not as other men. We are the saints of God and have the revelations of heaven. Where much is given much is expected. We are to put first in our lives the things of his kingdom." (Bruce R. McConkie, *Conference Report*, April 1975, p. 76.)

In addition to tithing, members of The Church of Jesus Christ of Latter-day Saints have other financial obligations in contributing to the building up of the kingdom of God. One of the Savior's commandments is to care for the poor and the needy. Jesus said that in the day of judgment he will separate the righteous from the wicked, "as a shepherd divideth his sheep from the goats." The separation will be determined by whether or not one gave assistance to those in need. If one assists the poor and the sick, it is tantamount to doing the same for the Savior. An inheritance in the kingdom of God will be prepared for those who follow this commandment, while those who do not will be cast away into punishment. (Matthew 25:31-46.)

An example of Jesus' teachings regarding the necessity to help those in need was his counsel to the rich young ruler: "If thou wilt be perfect, go and sell that thou hast, and give to the poor, and thou shalt have treasure in heaven: and come and follow me." (Matthew 19:21.)

Similarly, emphasis has been placed by Jesus on caring for those in need in this dispensation: "And remember in all things the poor and the needy, the sick and the afflicted, for he that doeth not these things, the same is not my disciple." (D&C 52:40.) The disciple is he who follows the teachings of the Master to which he is bound by the baptismal covenant. (D&C 41:5.) Baptism of the water and of the Spirit gives remission of sins so that the convert might go forward on the road to eventual exaltation. Since everyone sins to some degree after baptism, the sincere member of Christ's church desires to so live that he is as blameless as mortality will permit. The prophet Benjamin taught the following regarding the baptismal covenant: "And now, for the sake of these things which I have spoken unto you—that is, for the sake of retaining a remission of your sins from day to day, that ye may walk guiltless before God—I would that ye should impart of your sub-stance to the poor, every man according to that which he hath, such as feeding the hungry, clothing the naked, visiting the sick and administering to their relief, both spiritually and temporally, according to their wants." (Mosiah 4:26.)

Does the Lord require us to sell all of our possessions and give them to the poor, as he commanded the rich young ruler? Elder Bruce R. McConkie contemplated the results of the young man's decision: "And we are left to wonder what intimacies he might have shared with the Son of God, what fellowship he might have enjoyed with the apostles, what revelations and visions he might have received, if he had been *able* to live the law of a celestial kingdom. As it is he remains nameless; as it might have been, his name could have been had in honorable remembrance among the saints forever." (*Conference Report,* April 1975, p. 76.)

There are circumstances that require that one give everything, if necessary, for the establishment of Zion, such as under the law of consecration. At present, however, the members of the Church are under the same covenant as the people of King Benjamin's day—to impart of each one's substance "according to that which he hath." (Mosiah 4:26.) Regarding this commandment, Benja-min said that it should be "done in wisdom and order; for it is not requisite that a man should run faster than he has strength," but he must be diligent. (Mosiah 4:27.)

Every member of the Church is a steward over his possessions, and the day will come when he must give an accounting of his stewardship. The Lord has provided us with the breath of life and all that we have. We are promised that it is his purpose to provide for his people, but "it must needs be done in mine own way." What is the Lord's way? It is by exalting the poor, "in that the rich are made low." (D&C 104:11-16.) The Lord has given this warn-ing to his people: "Therefore, if any man shall take of the abun-dance which I have made, and impart not his portion, according to the law of my gospel, unto the poor and the needy, he shall, with the wicked, lift up his eyes in hell, being in torment." (D&C 104:18.) At the day of judgment, the rich who will not give to the poor will lament that "the harvest is past, the summer is ended, and my soul is not saved!" (D&C 56: 16.) All of us are agents to do 83 with our stewardships as we choose, but as the covenant people of God we are directed by revelation from the prophets as to what we should do. We need not be led astray by the ideas of men, for we can find security in following the Lord's way.

What is the Lord's plan to take care of the poor and the needy? He has provided the way by which the Saints may be consistent in their obedience to this law and at the same time show their loyalty to his servants who are charged with the responsibility of dispensing help to those in need. The revelations place the responsibility upon the Church to take care of its poor when relatives' means are not forthcoming. The Lord's agents, bishops and branch presidents, under the direction of the President of the Church, who is the Trustee-in-Trust for the Church, are to care for the funds used to help the poor. Members of the Church are to be full tithe payers. They are also to contribute fast offerings and make welfare donations of labor and money.

The law of the fast, which includes the payment of fast offerings, is officially defined as follows: "Proper observance of the monthly fast consists of going without food and drink for two consecutive meals, attending the fast and testimony meeting, and making a generous offering to the bishop for the care of those in need. This generous offering is the fast offering." (*General Handbook of Instructions*, Number 21 [1976], pp. 91-92.)

Early in this dispensation the Saints were commanded to fast. (D&C 59:7-14.) One Sunday of each month members congregate in fast and testimony meetings, having fasted as prescribed, and worship the Lord by partaking of the sacrament, singing, and bearing witness of his goodness to them. President David O. McKay taught that fasting "produces (1) physical benefits; (2) intellectual activity; and (3) spiritual strength." Regarding the latter, he said that fasting gives "all the spiritual uplift that comes from a Christlike desire to serve one's fellow man" and an economic means by which the needs of the worthy poor in the Church can be supplied. Associated with this practice is the divine service expressed in the Savior's words: "Inasmuch as ye have done it unto one of the least of these my brethren, ye have done it unto me. (Matthew 25:40.)" (*Gospel Ideals*, pp. 209-10.)

The value of the practice of fasting and contributing a fast offering has been well expressed by President McKay: "If we

84   contribute to the bishop the value of two meals once a month, we are certainly no poorer financially than we would be if we had consumed those meals as we regularly do. There cannot be any loss to our own family in a financial way, and we have given at least a mite towards alleviation of hunger, perhaps distress, in some home that is less fortunate, less blessed than we. There is no loss to us financially, no man is poorer, no man is deprived of one blessing, no child is deprived of anything that he would have had if he refrained from giving that small contribution. Financially then, nobody who gives it is any the poorer." (Ibid., p. 211.)

    In 1936 the Church inaugurated the welfare program to assist the worthy poor through agricultural and other projects, the products of which would be distributed by the bishop. Helping the worthy poor includes more than giving food and other necessities. The intent of the program is to eliminate idleness by establishing independence, industry, thrift, and self-respect. To help the individual help himself is a main factor in this plan. Again, the giving of one's skills, labor, and means for the benefit of those in need contributes to one's spiritual welfare.

    Not all wards and stakes have welfare projects, especially those that have been organized recently. Fast offering funds become the means of alleviating want in places where the welfare program is not fully functioning. Fast offerings are also used in the welfare program for necessities that are not produced in that system. All members need to contribute generously to the fast offering funds to take care of those who lack the necessities of life. A challenge was given to the membership of the Church by President Marion G. Romney, counselor in the First Presidency, who admonished us to accept the Lord's promise of prosperity given through the prophet Malachi (Malachi 3:7-12.): "If you here today would like to test this promise, double your fast offerings and pay more than a tithing this year. My own experience is that the Lord keeps His promises." (*Conference Report,* October 1974, p. 171.)

    The Book of Mormon prophet Amulek counseled the Nephites to have faith unto repentance and to pray diligently to the Lord over their homes and flocks and for "the welfare of those who are around you." (Alma 34:15-27.) Prayers are in vain, however, if one does not follow the commandment to care for the poor: "And now behold, my beloved brethren, I say unto you, do not suppose that this is all; for after ye have done all these things, if ye turn away the needy, and the naked, and visit not the sick and afflicted, and impart of your substance, if ye have, to those who stand in need—I say unto you, if ye do not any of these things, behold, your prayer is vain, and availeth you nothing, and ye are as hypocrites who do deny the faith." (Alma 34:28.)

Every faithful Latter-day Saint should be anxious to do everything possible for his own salvation and that of others. Salvation comes through works of righteousness as well as faith and prayers. As people join the Church through the missionary effort, they are given more opportunities to participate in salvation practices. Their opportunity to serve the poor in the Lord's way becomes a reality as they are faithful in keeping the commandments. The contribution of their means, even the minimum contribution, moves the work of the Lord onward. President Spencer W. Kimball suggested that their contribution be in proportion to their affluence:

"We do not have projects in all the world, as we are expanding so rapidly in the overseas areas. We haven't established farms and other projects there as we have here, but there is no reason why the latest organized branch cannot take care of itself in large measure if we pay our fast offerings. Sometimes we have been a bit penurious and figured that we had for breakfast one egg and that cost so many cents and then we give that to the Lord. I think that when we are affluent, as many of us are, that we ought to be very, very generous.

". . . I think we should be very generous and give, instead of the amount we saved by our two meals of fasting, perhaps much, much more—ten times more where we are in a position to do it. I know there are some who couldn't." (*Conference Report*, April 1974, p. 184.)

When we consider all aspects of life in the light of our eternal existence, there can be but one conclusion regarding the privilege of consecrating our time, talents, and means to the Lord's work. Life is as a speck of time when compared with the eternity ahead, which is an endless period of joyful living in the celestial kingdom for those whose efforts are centered in the Lord's plan. As Elder Bruce R. McConkie said:

"We can pay an honest tithing and contribute to our fast offering, welfare, budget, building, and missionary funds. We can bequeath portions of our assets and devise portions of our proper-

86   ties to the Church when we pass on to other spheres. . . .

"But the work of the kingdom must go forward, and the members of the Church are and shall be called upon to bear off its burdens. It is the Lord's work and not man's. He is the one who commands us to preach the gospel in all the world, whatever the cost. . . . He is the one who tells us to care for the poor among us, whatever the cost, lest their cries come up to his throne as a testimony against those who should have fed the hungry and clothed the naked but who did not.

"And may I say also—both by way of doctrine and of testimony—that it is his voice which invites us to consecrate of our time, our talents, and our means to carry on his work. It is his voice that calls for service and sacrifice. This is his work. He is at the helm guiding and directing the destiny of his kingdom.

"And every member of his church has this promise: That if he remains true and faithful—obeying, serving, consecrating, sacrificing, as required by the gospel—he shall be repaid in eternity a thousandfold and shall have eternal life. What more can we ask?" (*Conference Report,* April 1975, pp. 76-77.)

12

OUR DUTY AS LATTER-DAY SAINTS

The Church of Jesus Christ of Latter-day Saints came into existence by revelation from God as predicted by biblical prophets. (Acts 3:19-21; Ephesians 1:8-10; Revelation 14:6-7.) Since the day when Joseph Smith received the vision of the Eternal Father and his Son Jesus Christ, revelation to those who have presided over the Church has been continuous. The Prophet Joseph received by revelation the doctrines and teachings of the gospel of Jesus Christ necessary for the salvation of all. Since the organization of the Church on April 6, 1830, the Lord's will has been made manifest to the prophets and the members through the power of the Holy Ghost. Through this power everyone may know for himself that the modern revelations are of God. Hundreds of thousands have borne witness that the blessings of obedience to the counsel of the Lord's servants are received. Among the fundamental laws of the gospel that have been proved a great blessing, both temporally and spiritually, is tithing. Tithe payers have come to know that both giver and receiver are blessed greatly.

Fundamental to an organized body of people is the need for revenue to take care of the objectives of that group. The Lord instituted the law of tithing and offerings anciently and has restored this law so that his kingdom might eventually develop to fill the whole earth. At times the offerings have been in kind—animals and grains and so forth—as in the early days of the Church, when money was scarce and barter in other media of exchange was more common. At the present time members are counseled to pay tithing in the common medium of exchange. Each Latter-day Saint is expected to attend an annual tithing settlement interview with his bishop or branch president. This interview gives the donor an opportunity to indicate his understanding of the amount he has contributed during the year and to indicate whether or not he is a full tithe payer. The financial record of the ward or branch is kept in the Church archives for use by Church leaders when necessary. There is another purpose for keeping this record. During the days of the law of consecration the

88 Lord revealed that there should be a history maintained of all things that transpired in Zion, including the members' "manner of life, their faith, and works." (D&C 85:1-2.) The intent was that the law of consecration be lived, "that he may tithe his people, to prepare them against the day of vengeance and burning." (D&C 85:3.) Those who were unprepared or were apostates were not to have their genealogy kept "or to be had where it may be found on any of the records or history of the church." Furthermore, their names and those of their children were not to be "written in the book of the law of God." (D&C 85:4-5.) President Joseph Fielding Smith wrote the following about this record: "The book of the law of God was the book to be kept by the Lord's clerk. There is also another book which is kept in heaven, and the one kept in heaven, and the one kept by the Lord's clerk should be accurately kept so that it would agree with the Lamb's Book of Life. (D&C 128:7.) In the Lamb's Book of Life only the names are received of those who have washed their garments white 'in the blood of the Lamb.' This is in harmony with the word of the Lord to John. . . . (Revelation 21:27.)" (*Church History and Modern Revelation*, 1953, 1:349.)

The records on the earth and in heaven will form the basis for judgment in that day when the Lord shall make up his jewels. During the first decade of the Church's existence in this dispensation, the law of consecration was instituted to provide for the temporal and spiritual welfare of the Saints. Due to the transgression of the people in not observing the covenant of consecration, the Saints in Jackson County, Missouri, were driven by mobs from "the land of their inheritance." Their chastening and trial was necessary, even as Abraham was tried when commanded to offer up his son Isaac. (D&C 101:1-5; 105:1-6.)

To become legal heirs of inheritances on this earth when it becomes a celestial kingdom, we not only must believe in the teachings of the gospel, but we also must live them. To be one of the "pure in heart," we must live by the commandments so that we may be sanctified, even as the land is sanctified by the payment of tithing. Elder Melvin J. Ballard explained: "Do we not hope and expect to have an inheritance in the celestial kingdom, even upon this earth in its redeemed and sanctified state? What are the terms under which we may obtain that inheritance? The law of tithing is the law of inheritance. It leads to it. No man may hope or expect to have an inheritance on this celestial globe who has failed to pay his tithing. By the payment of his honest tithing he is establishing a right and a title to this inheritance, and he cannot secure it upon any other terms but by complying with this and other just requirements; and this is one of the very essential things." (*Conference Report,* October 1929, p. 51.)

How would you like to inherit a land rich with "milk and honey, upon which there shall be no curse"? (D&C 38:16-18.) The land of your inheritance will be for you and "your children forever, while the earth shall stand, and ye shall possess it again in eternity, no more to pass away." (D&C 38: 19-20.)

Is not the foregoing a part of the answer to the question, Is a person blessed who pays an honest tithing and other donations? As we read the testimonies of those who have prospered materially through keeping the commandments, we learn that temporal blessings do not necessarily include an abundance of wealth. The experience of the faithful Saints is that they are sustained temporally, but the greatest blessings are spiritual because they include the present and eternity. Though one may not have riches equal with the wealthy of the earth, the greatest wealth is exaltation in the celestial kingdom. The things of lasting value are those which bring happiness here and eternal joys. In harmony with this thought Elder Rudger Clawson said of one who had prospered greatly in wealth but who had not paid his offerings to the Lord: "Do you think that man will prosper? One may say, yes, he is prospering, and getting lots of grain and potatoes; he is building barns, and so on, and he is widening out, and he is multiplying in his stock, and property and all. Do you say he is blessed? Go into his home, and you will find out what kind of a spirit is there. See if there is a spirit of love, a spirit of knowledge, a spirit of faith? That is what you should look for and see if the man is blessed or not? Why, these very riches that he has obtained may be a curse to him, may canker his soul and destroy it." (*Conference Report,* October 1913, pp. 56-57.)

The teachings of the prophets have always been to accept the Lord's promise that he will open "the windows of heaven, and pour you out a blessing, that there shall not be room enough to receive it." (Malachi 3:10.) Effective faith in the Lord's words brings obedience to his commandments. As we draw nearer to the Lord, he will answer according to what is best for us. "Draw near

90

unto me and I will draw near unto you; seek me diligently and ye shall find me; ask, and ye shall receive; knock, and it shall be opened unto you. Whatsoever ye ask the Father in my name it shall be given unto you, that is expedient for you; And if ye ask anything that is not expedient for you, it shall turn unto your condemnation." (D&C 88:63-65.)

How do we know what is good or expedient for us? By living so close to the Lord that our prayers are answered in inspiring guidance. President Joseph F. Smith's faith and experience was such that he could give the following counsel:

"It is the purpose of God in restoring the gospel and the holy Priesthood not only to benefit mankind spiritually, but also to benefit them temporally. The Lord has expressed this many times, in the word that he gave to his servant Joseph Smith, the prophet; he designed that his people should become the richest of all people. And this not only means the richest of all people in heavenly gifts—in spiritual blessings and riches, but it also means that the people of God shall be the richest of all people with regard to temporal matters. If faithful, we have a right to claim the blessings of the Lord upon the labor of our hands, our temporal labors. The farmer has a right to ask the Lord for blessings upon his farm, upon the labor that he bestows upon it. He has a right to claim the blessings of the Lord upon the animals that are necessary to the cultivation of his farm. He has a right to ask God to bless the grain that he sows and the seeds of the fruit that he plants in the soil. It is his privilege, not only to ask and claim these blessings at the hand of the Lord, but it is his right and privilege to receive blessings from God upon his labor, upon his farm, and upon all that he puts his hand unto in righteousness. It is our privilege to ask God to remove the curse from the earth, and to make it fruitful. If we will live so that we shall be entitled to his favor, and so that we may justly and righteously claim the blessings and gifts that he has promised unto his Saints, then that which we ask will be given, and we shall receive and enjoy them more abundantly. It is our privilege to ask God to bless the elements that surround us and to temper them for our good, and we know he will hear and answer the prayers of his people, according to their faith." (*Gospel Doctrine*, p. 209.)

The Lord has placed high priority upon the blessing of peace of mind and heart. He gave the prescription on how to receive "peace in this world, and eternal life in the world to come." Only through works of righteousness can we receive peace. (D&C 59:23.) "Listen to my words," "clothe yourselves with the bond of charity, as with a mantle, which is the bond of perfectness and peace." (D&C 19:23; 88:125.) How well these words describe obedience to the law of tithing and offerings— "works of righteousness"—or the multitude of blessings given to others through offerings. "The bond of charity," defined as love and almsgiving, also fits the law of tithes and offerings. All Latter-day Saints who have experienced the joy that comes from walking in obedience to the words of the Lord and the living prophets know "the peace of God which passeth all understanding." (Philippians 4:7.) There is a soul satisfaction in being on the Lord's side of the line. Dr. Ernest L. Wilkinson related the following experience of the late Fred G. Taylor to illustrate the satisfaction that comes to one who is honest with the Lord and his fellowmen:

"As a young man he had rather spectacular financial success. Like many young men who have success of that kind, he became self-reliant and felt that he could manage his own affairs without further help of the Lord. Consequently, although he had a large income, he forgot to render an account unto the Lord. But at the end of World War I when he had large investments in sugar stocks, he was caught in a squeeze in the market; and the first thing he knew, he ended up not only having lost his entire fortune, but some $52,000 in debt. Because of a mistake of business judgment on his part, he had also caused his company to sustain a severe loss, and he was discharged from his position.

"He went home that night broken hearted and reported to his sweet wife what had happened to them. Much to his surprise, she said, 'Fred, I have had an intuition that something like this would happen. We haven't been living close to the Lord. We are going to have to go back to our little country home on the farm and start again from scratch, but this time I want your promise that every cent of money we take in will be properly tithed.'

"Fred G. Taylor thereupon turned over to his creditors what was at that time one of the most pretentious homes in Ogden [Utah], went back to Harrisville [Utah], and started all over again in a little frame house on a small farm. Later, when through proper living he had re-established himself, he was elected head of Sugar Institute, Inc., in New York City, which was the national trade association for all sugar companies in the country. While there he became president of the New York Stake, a man loved and respected by every member of the Church in that part of the Lord's vineyard. That was some fifteen years after his financial debacle, but he was still paying his previous debts.

"One day he came to my office on Broadway, near Wall Street, where I was practicing law. President [Heber J.] Grant was along with him. President Taylor said he was getting together a few of his very close friends, whom he wanted to take to dinner that evening to tell them an important story, and I was invited. When we sat down to dinner that night, President Taylor proceeded to tell the story that I have just related to you, concluding that this was the happiest day of his life, because he had just paid off the last of his debts; and not only that, he had gone back and paid tithing on much of the income which he had lost in the depression following World War I. He had much more soul satisfaction that night than he could have had if he had accumulated millions." ("The Principle and Practice of Paying Tithing," *Brigham Young University Bulletin*, vol. 54, no. 25, December 10, 1957, pp. 12-13.)

Every person who pays tithing and fast offerings has the satisfaction of knowing that he is contributing to the phenomenal growth of the Church. He knows that the prophecies concerning the eventual triumph of the kingdom of God are due, in part, to his obedience, for he joins the numerous other faithful members as a participant in the fulfillment of ancient and modern predictions. The Church of Jesus Christ of Latter-day Saints is the kingdom of God on the earth, never to be destroyed, nor left to another people, "and it shall stand forever." (Daniel 2:44.) Modern prophecy is as explicit in this same declaration. (D&C 65:2; 109:72.) When mobs drove the Saints from their homes in Jackson County, Missouri, in 1834, the Lord revealed to his Prophet that the Saints would prevail against their enemies, and they would eventually receive an inheritance upon the earth if they were faithful in observing their covenants. (D&C 103:5-8.) With the passing years the fulfillment of this prophecy has continued until today the Saints, despite the efforts of the wicked, are witnessing the expansion of the Church throughout the world. The Church will continue to flourish, because there will be a sufficient number of members who will be striving to "observe all the words" that the Lord has given.

The obedient do not "resist the voice of the Lord" when he speaks through his prophets. The counsel the Lord gave to a member of the Church who had resisted his voice is intended for all members with the same inclination. (D&C 108.) When the still, small voice whispers to us to keep the commandments, including the payment of tithing and other offerings, and we ignore it in favor of spending the Lord's money for some pleasure or to gain material advantage, we resist the voice of the Lord. He counsels us to strengthen those who preside over us, in all our doings. (D&C 108:7.)

They who keep their covenants with the Lord will find security against the enticings of the evil one. They will stand secure in that day when the predicted judgments come upon the wicked. (D&C 29:13-21; 45:24-35.) Today is the time for obedience in giving our hearts to the Lord. This is the "day of sacrifice, and a day for the tithing of my people; for he that is tithed shall not be burned at his coming." (D&C 64:23.) What does that mean? Elder Rudger Clawson answered: "Does it mean that if a man will not pay his tithing, that the Lord is going to send a ball of fire down from heaven and burn him up? No; the Lord does not do that way. The Lord works on natural principles. This is what it means, if I read correctly: a man who ignores the express command of the Lord, by failing to pay his tithing, it means that the Spirit of the Lord will withdraw from him; it means that the power of the priesthood will withdraw from that man, if he continues in the spirit of neglect to do his duty. He will drift away into darkness, gradually but surely, until finally (mark you) he will lift up his eyes among the wicked. That is where he will finally land; and then when the destruction comes and when the burning comes, he will be among the wicked, and will be destroyed; while those who observe the law will be found among the righteous, and they will be preserved. There is a God in heaven, and He has promised to shield and protect them. I tell you there is a day of burning, a day of destruction coming upon the wicked. And where will we be? Will we be with the wicked, or with the righteous?" (*Conference Report*, October 1913, p. 59.)

The loss of the Holy Spirit, the gift that we have received by the laying on of hands, comes gradually as we resist the voice of the Lord, knowing that vows and covenants are not being lived. Meek and edifying language and even prayers are not effectual for salvation if we do not obey the voice of the Lord. (D&C 52:14-20.)

The companionship of the Holy Ghost is the wonderful blessing of the faithful. This blessing will secure us against loss of faith and apostasy, said President Heber C. Kimball:

"This Church has before it many close places through which it will have to pass before the work of God is crowned with victory. To meet the difficulties that are coming, it will be necessary for you to have a knowledge of the truth of this work for yourselves. The difficulties will be of such a character that the man or woman who does not possess this personal knowledge or witness will fall. If you have not got the testimony, live right and call upon the Lord and cease not till you obtain it. If you do not you will not stand.

"Remember these sayings, for many of you will live to see them fulfilled. The time will come when no man nor woman will be able to endure on borrowed light. Each will have to be guided by the light within himself. If you do not have it, how can you stand? Do you believe it?" (Orson F. Whitney, *Life of Heber C. Kimball,* pp. 449-50.)

"Therefore," the Lord declared, "let your hearts be comforted; for all things shall work together for good to them that walk uprightly, and to the sanctification of the church.

"For I will raise up unto myself a pure people, that will serve me in righteousness;

"And all that call upon the name of the Lord, and keep his commandments, shall be saved. Even so. Amen." (D&C 100:15-17.)

After all, is not this the purpose of our entering into a covenant relationship with the Lord? A "pure person," one who has received the atonement of Christ for his individual salvation and who serves the Lord diligently to the end, has come out of the bondage of sin (spiritual death) into spiritual life. (D&C 29:41-45.) When we break covenants through disobedience, the loss of the Spirit removes the protection that helped and assisted us to overcome our enemies. From Elder Rudger Clawson we learn: "The lines are being drawn. It must be known to the authorities of this Church and to the people who are faithful and who are not faithful. God requires it and it must be recorded, for the reason plainly set forth in the revelation, that those whose names are not found recorded in the book of the law of God shall have no inheritance in Zion in that day when our eternal inheritances shall be divided out to us." (*Conference Report,* April 1900, pp. 43-44.)

Remember also that the Lord's words to the Prophet Joseph Smith are just as applicable today as when they were given:

"But remember, God is merciful; therefore, repent of that which thou hast done which is contrary to the commandment which I gave you, and thou art still chosen, and art again called to the work;

"Except thou do this, thou shalt be delivered up and become as other men, and have no more gift." (D&C 3:10-11.)

BIBLIOGRAPHY

Articles, Periodicals, Miscellaneous

Conference Report. Salt Lake City: The Church of Jesus Christ of Latter-day Saints. Proceedings of annual and semiannual conferences of The Church of Jesus Christ of Latter-day Saints.

Journal of Discourses. 26 vols. Sermons delivered by various leaders of The Church of Jesus Christ of Latter-day Saints. 1854-1886. Published in Liverpool, England.

Millennial Star. Liverpool, England.

New Era. Monthly youth magazine of The Church of Jesus Christ of Latter-day Saints.

Shoemaker, Donald P. "Why Your Neighbor Joined the Mormon Church." *Christianity Today,* October 11, 1974, pp. 11-12, 15.

Joseph Smith. *Lectures on Faith.*

Snow, LeRoi C. "From Despair to Freedom Through Tithing." *Deseret News,* Church News, March 29, 1941, pp. 5-6, 8.

————. "The Lord's Way Out of Bondage." *Improvement Era,* July 1938, pp. 400ff.

Speeches of the Year. Provo, Utah: Brigham Young University Extension Publications, 1961.

Talks delivered at the Welfare Agricultural Meeting, October 3, 1970.

The Ten Commandments Today. Salt Lake City: General Board of the Mutual Improvement Associations, M-Man-Gleaner Manual, 1954-55.

Wilkinson, Ernest L. "The Principle and Practice of Paying Tithing." *Brigham Young University Bulletin,* 54:25, December 10, 1957.

Books

Cannon, George Q. *Gospel Truth,* comp. Jerreld L. Newquist. 2 vols. Salt Lake City: Deseret Book Co., 1974.

Clark, James R., comp. *Messages of the First Presidency*, vol. 4. Salt Lake City: Bookcraft, 1970.

Grant, Heber J. *Gospel Standards*, comp. G. Homer Durham. Salt Lake City: Improvement Era, 1969.

McKay, David O. *Gospel Ideals*. Salt Lake City: Improvement Era, 1953.

Nibley, Preston, comp. *Inspirational Talks for Youth*. Salt Lake City: Deseret Book Co., 1965.

Romney, Thomas C. *The Life of Lorenzo Snow*. Salt Lake City: Deseret News, 1955.

Smith, George Albert. *Sharing the Gospel with Others*, comp. Preston Nibley. Salt Lake City: Deseret News Press, 1950.

Smith, Joseph. *History of the Church of Jesus Christ of Latter-day Saints*, ed. B. H. Roberts. 7 vols. Salt Lake City: The Church of Jesus Christ of Latter-day Saints.

———. *Teachings of the Prophet Joseph Smith*, comp. Joseph Fielding Smith. Salt Lake City: Deseret Book Co., 1976.

Smith, Joseph F. *Gospel Doctrine*, comp. Joseph Fielding Smith. Salt Lake City: Deseret Book Co., 1970.

Smith, Joseph Fielding. *Answers to Gospel Questions*, vol. 3. Salt Lake City: Deseret Book Co., 1970.

———. *Church History and Modern Revelation*. 2 vols. Salt Lake City: Deseret Book Co., 1953.

———. *Doctrines of Salvation*, comp. Bruce R. McConkie. 2 vols. Salt Lake City: Bookcraft, 1974.

Talmage, James E. *The Articles of Faith*. Salt Lake City: Deseret Book Co., 1966.

Taylor, John. *Gospel Kingdom*, comp. G. Homer Durham. Salt Lake City: Bookcraft, 1964.

Whitney, Orson F. *Life of Heber C. Kimball*. Salt Lake City: Bookcraft, 1967.

Widtsoe, John A. *Joseph Smith: Seeker After Truth, Prophet of God*. Salt Lake City: Bookcraft, 1957.

Woodruff, Wilford. *Discourses of Wilford Woodruff*, comp. G. Homer Durham. Salt Lake City: Bookcraft, 1946.

Young, Brigham. *Discourses of Brigham Young*, comp. John A. Widtsoe. Salt Lake City: Deseret Book Co., 1973.

INDEX